Speculative Realism
An Epitome

Leon Niemoczynski

Kismet Press
MMXVII | Epitomes II

Speculative Realism

AN EPITOME

Leon Niemoczynski

kismet·press

Libera Scientia | Free Knowledge

Speculative Realism: An Epitome
by Leon Niemoczynski

Epitomes, 2
Series Editors: Tim Barnwell & N. Kıvılcım Yavuz

Published in 2017
by Kismet Press LLP
15 Queen Square, Leeds, LS2 8AJ, UK
kismet.press
kismet@kismet.press

Copyright © 2017 Leon Niemoczynski

Published by Kismet Press LLP under an exclusive license to publish. Commercial copying, hiring, lending is prohibited. The book is freely available online at <kismet.press> under a Creative Commons Attribution-NonCommercial-NoDerivatives 4.0 International (CC BY-NC-ND 4.0) license. See <https://creativecommons.org/licenses/by-nc-nd/4.0/> for details.

Downloadable .epub edition also available

Printed and bound by IngramSpark with acid-free paper, using a print-on-demand model with printers in the US, EU, and Australia

A catalogue record for this book is available from the British Library

ISBN 978-0-9956717-5-1 (pbk)
ISBN 978-0-9956717-6-8 (ebk)

Contents

Acknowledgments	vii
Introduction	1
0.1 An Epitome	1
0.2 From Mourning to Celebrating the Death of Speculative Realism	3
0.3 Varying Streams and Currents "after the Speculative Turn"	4
0.4 The New Metaphysics: A Scene Report	13
0.5 A General, Non-Technical Introduction	18
Resources for Further Reading	19
Notes	20
I Dead on Arrival	21
1.1 What Is Speculative Realism?	21
1.2 A Review of the Literature and a Short History of Speculative Realism	28
1.3 Why Discuss Speculative Realism?	34
1.4 Reading the Rites of Burial	39
Resources for Further Reading	41
Notes	42

II Heirs of Kantian Finitude — 43
2.1 The Subject at Center — 43
2.2 Metaphysics before Kant — 48
2.3 Metaphysics after Kant — 54
2.4 From Finitude to Perspectivalism and Anti-Realism — 57
Resources for Further Reading — 65
Notes — 66

III After Finitude — 67
3.1 Correlationism and the Goal of *After Finitude* — 67
3.2 Strong and Weak Correlationism — 75
3.3 Breaking with the Circle of Correlation: Facticity and Arche-Fossil — 85
3.4 Mathematics Attaining the Unthought — 92
Resources for Further Reading — 107
Notes — 108

IV After Nature — 111
4.1 Speculative Nihilism/Transcendental Realism in *Nihil Unbound* — 111
4.2 Speculative Idealism/Transcendental Materialism in *Philosophies of Nature after Schelling* — 121
4.3 Conclusion — 132
Resources for Further Reading — 136
Notes — 137

Interview with Ray Brassier — 139

Interview with Iain Hamilton Grant — 161

Credits — 183

Acknowledgments

RAY BRASSIER AND IAIN HAMILTON GRANT BOTH HAVE been wonderful in agreeing to offer me the opportunity to interview with them just a few years ago. Both have been nothing but cordial, helpful, and professional in our interactions since and so I should certainly offer my thanks to each of them first and foremost. Ray especially has been kind enough to refer my name to others as a specialist in the field (bringing about professional opportunities as a result) and for that I am most thankful. Many thanks are also in order to one Quentin Meillassoux who has answered email correspondences however briefly, taking time out of his busy schedule to do so.

Pete Wolfendale, Jason Hills, Terence Blake, Ben Woodward, Bryan "Skholiast," Dirk Felleman, Charles Klayman, Louis Morelle, and Adrian Ivakhiv have been productive online interlocutors throughout the years as has the P.E.S.T. organization been in person, especially Karen Oyama and Jason Bell. Thanks so much for the great conversations and sharing of ideas. John Caputo has also been a productive interlocutor both through email correspondence and in person regarding many of the ideas that I discuss in this book.

For personal encouragement and guidance as well as incisive insight I would like to thank Robert S. Corrington and Marilynn Lawrence. They both have helped me to see how Continental realism and materialism might fit within the perspective of philosophical naturalism. During my time at Immaculata University Stephanie Theodorou was always so selfless and gracious in her role as friend, collaborator, and colleague. I owe much of my comprehension of Hegel and Malabou exclusively to her. Arash Naraghi, Carol Moeller, and Bernie Cantens, all colleagues at Moravian College, deserve my gratitude and thanks for being supportive of my scholarship (and teaching) as well. I thank them for providing a stimulating and rewarding environment in which my current outlook can continue to grow and bloom.

I would also very much like to acknowledge and thank my students at Moravian College for remaining to be the most energizing part of my writing process. At the time of this book's publication there will have been at least two "Continental philosophy" seminars that I have taught where speculative realism was a unit to be covered. It was through the reactions of my students that I was able to gauge the strength of ideas I intended to include or exclude in this book. Justly then, *they* were the final gate-keepers. I am excited for such wonderful and bright students to help me in future seminars continue to write new projects and test ideas. Some of these forthcoming writings will most certainly stem from the open spirit of speculation found in the work of such thinkers as Ray Brassier, Iain Grant, and Quentin Meillassoux. I am very optimistic as to where these ideas may be able to go and what life they may take.

Lastly but most importantly my wife, Nalina, has been incredibly patient with and supportive of my writing this manuscript. It proved to be quite difficult (and time consuming) for as short of a project that I imagined it to be. However, she was there to cheer me on as always.

Introduction

0.1 An Epitome

An "epitome" can be defined as an "exemplification, typification, or quintessence." Regarding "speculative realism" I do not mean to write "a perfect example of a particular quality or type" but only to offer an abstract of its brief life before moving on to discuss three of what I consider to be the most emblematic philosophers of the recent speculative turn in Continental philosophy. Those philosophers are Ray Brassier, Iain Hamilton Grant, and Quentin Meillassoux. Of course many other names could have been placed in this book and by mentioning only a few I am sure I would omit many more. However, to me, at the very least, these three philosophers ought to be written about so as to characterize the milieu of contemporary Continental speculative philosophy for those interested to learn about it.

Indeed it is true that Ray Brassier has written what should be considered to be "the last word" regarding speculative realism and so, other than the first chapter of this book (a sort of "burial rites" for speculative realism whereas Brassier has already provided its "autopsy") I do not write about "Speculative Realism" proper or per se but about speculative, realist, and materialist philosophy in the 21st century; that is, what may be called "Continental realism and materialism," "new realism," "new materialism," or most generically "the new metaphysics." I must state that despite any title this book is written out of admiration and respect for the sheer philosophical strength of Brassier, Grant, and Meillassoux—this in addition to their courage to remain professionally distanced from the online immaturity which unfortunately has come to surround the initiation of a "speculative turn" in the world of professional academic philosophy. The general nature of their philosophy as picked up in contemporary academic circles therefore is here of importance rather than the histrionics which surrounds any name-branding of it.

There will more than likely be those who meet this book with silence, being unable to cope with the telling of the history of speculative realism as it truly occurred. Nevertheless, it is indeed now that there finally exists a published acknowledgment of Brassier's postscript "Speculative Autopsy" (as it is found in Pete Wolfendale's debut book) which has undoubtedly given "the last word" regarding any possible meaning of speculative realism. If I may be permitted to say, I believe that we ought to heed this last word—which declares that speculative realism does not index anything meaningfully cohesive and therefore cannot be claimed to somehow properly "exist"—for, after all, it was Brassier who coined the term, so his word concerning its meaning should stand.

0.2 From Mourning to Celebrating the Death of Speculative Realism

With that said I should straightaway be forthcoming about the first chapter of the present work. Other than the fact that, for me, a first chapter can be among the most difficult to write, a general overview of speculative realism requires that one discuss its history. Discussing this history is required because without understanding what caused the initial flash of Speculative Realism and how its initial promise was subdued one cannot understand what now comes "after" any so-called speculative turn. Thus, the first chapter of this book opens on perhaps what may be perceived as a fairly negative note simply because, unfortunately, the history of speculative realism, specifically the several-year-long battle which took place over the term's meaning, is quite negative. But, the telling of that tale is not without its promise. I attempt to close that first chapter on a more positive note by calling out how, rather than *mourn* the death of speculative realism we might actually choose to *celebrate* it, for even if speculative realism is no more (or never was) there still exists the opportunity to engender the sort of spirit which initiated the speculative turn to begin with. And with that I sincerely hope therefore that others will be able to disregard any brand or factional attachments and read the work of these philosophers for the sheer brilliance that it is: focus on the *ideas* in play and comment upon them, critique and assess them—or perhaps even critically incorporate them into one's own outlook and work. With a great degree of humility I can say that I have at least tried to do as much for the past ten years.

By the time this book has been published it will be ten years since the 2007 Speculative Realism workshop. While not much has come of the name, the brand, or of any "movement" being a distinct name referencing anything substantial that has secured a place in the canon of Continental philosophy (as existentialism, phenomenology, hermeneutics, and deconstruction have) still, speculation is in the air as there has been a general turn from the reigning *phenomenological* metaphysics of Continental philosophy to a *speculative*, realist, and materialist one. Indeed root has taken place within soil tilled by the 2007 Speculative Realism workshop that stretches and challenges what we mean by "Continental philosophy" as such.

0.3 Varying Streams and Currents "after the Speculative Turn"

In some ways growth from the soil of speculative realism has already occurred as new streams of thought that are all speculative, realist, and materialist in their metaphysics emerge. If pressed, what follows could be organized into four main strands, all of which are speculatively realist in orientation. These strands so-called are *materalistic*, *scientistic*, *naturalistic*, and *vitalistic*. Along another axis the four strands typically emphasize either *rationality* as speculative tool (including mathematical set theory, dialectics, non-standard analysis, categorial theory, abductive logic) or *aesthetical affect* as speculative tool (i.e., "feeling," "prehension," "allure," "affect" in aesthetics, communications and rhetoric, semiotics). Either rational or aesthetical method can be phenomenological or not (although as we shall see phenomenology undergoes a radical transformation). All streams are realist. All are speculative. Only some are systematic. It should be noted that these are not hard and fast distinctions but are offered merely as ways to think about how each of the below wings of the "post-speculative turn" differ from each other. But all have grown and profited from the speculative turn in some way or another.

For example, one stream of thinking is actually a predecessor to the 2007 Speculative Realism workshop and indeed influenced it: the advent of "Accelerationism," and today the subsequent creation of various related philosophical schools constituting a sort of neo-rationalism, are in dialogue with, if not creating anew, contemporary metaphysical discourse. Accelerationism could be described as ontological Promethean philosophy embracing science, technology, reason, and speed with the motto of "in and through," where, according to *#Accelerate: The Accelerationist Reader*, "Accelerationism is the name of a contemporary political heresy: the insistence that the only radical political response to capitalism is not to protest, disrupt, critique, or détourne it, but to accelerate and exacerbate its uprooting, alienating, decoding, abstractive tendencies." Thanks to the work of Ray Brassier, Nick Land is often connected with this new speculative philosophy as is the work of

Sadie Plant, Reza Negarastani, Pete Wolfendale, and the now defunct CCRU (the Cybernetic Culture Research Unit—an underground academic center which grew up in '80s apocalyptic sci-fi, rave, acid, cyberpunk culture). As it stands there are both "left" and "right" (NrX or "Neo-reactionary") strands of Accelerationism. But in each the result is the same, "nihilistic jouissance" and "mad black Deleuzianism." Nature shall have "no speed limit" as scientific rationality telescopically achieves a forthcoming technological singularity whose aim is the instant realization of intelligence and means of material production.

Still others experiment on the side of what has been called "New Materialism" (the edited volume *New Materialism: Interviews & Cartographies* charts these directions in cultural theory, feminism, science studies, and the arts, as does Cool and Frost's *New Materialisms: Ontology, Agency, and Politics*), where unlike before when Continental thought was wary of materialist thinking, materialism is now reconfigured and embraced: matter is seen as vitalistic, potent, and self-powering rather than dead, inert, and unproductive. Nature is taken to be "vibrant," offering through aesthetic modes of sensibility and communication "lines of insight" into its own infinitely creative and productive ground. Many take on the mantle of Catherine Malabou and her notion of "plasticity" to think about nature, matter, and culture and how they relate creatively to the objects of nature which create themselves as much as humans claim to create them. Scholars in this field could include Karen Barad, Rosi Braidotti, Jussi Parikka, Brian Massumi, and Erin Manning. For New Materialism, "matter feels, converses, suffers, desires, yearns, and remembers."[1] Principal influences are Deleuze, Whitehead, Bergson, Gabriel Tarde, and Gilbert Simondon. The focus is on nature's objects understood as self-creative *agents* rather than upon any general ground of creativity and activity as such. In this New Materialism is closely related to Bruno Latour's "actor-network" theory that treats whatever particulars there are as agents or "actors" within social networks.

On the other side of this "bright" form of new materialism there is, roughly, its darker side, or "Dark Materialism"—sometimes called "Dark Vitalism," "Cosmic Pessimism," or "Cosmicism." Taking cue from both Brassier and Meillassoux, authors such as Eugene Thacker or Ben Woodward craft ontologies that celebrate a reality-without-human and attempt to intelligently own up to our inevitable extinction and loss of place within the universe (pace Brassier's *Nihil Unbound*). Thacker tells us, "There is a logic of pessimism that is fundamental to its suspicion of philosophical system. Pessimism involves a statement about a condition. In pessimism each statement boils down to an affirmation or a negation, just as any condition boils down to the best or the worst." And the conclusion? "We're doomed." Drawing upon Schopenhauer, Nietzsche, Cioran, H.P. Lovecraft, and a good dose of theory present in the first season of HBO's *True Detective*, Dark Materialism/Cosmicism is a yes-saying to the indifference of the cosmos and a no-saying to the "for-us." This wing of speculative philosophy is no foe to the rational or physical sciences in its embrace of the sort of enlightenment required for human beings to fully comprehend that the universe will gladly go on once we are gone. Science reveals the *truth* of the matter which is a truth concerning *human extinction*.

Scientifically regarding this indifferent universe and its cosmic darkness, long-time speculative philosopher Francois Laruelle has invoked his "non-standard philosophy," so as to stand against the brightness lit by any vibrant center prized by New Materialists. For Laruelle, "philosophers are children who are afraid of the dark." Himself in dialogue with Deleuze and today with Badiou and Brassier Laruelle is still mostly a minority figure within Continental metaphysics if only because of his opaque style. But, his speculative, realist ontology is ambitious. Laruelle seeks to define the essence of multiplicities where his Absolute admits difference "deeply" as an "in-One." For him, ontological difference is not relative but is continuous among and between multiplicities such that multiplicities are not "static" but are always immanently "in relation" to an in-One, thus a "deep" monism. About Laruelle's deep monism French philosopher of science and ontological pluralist Terence Blake writes "The Absolute is not won through active and willful negation, but is attained more passively and patiently, by letting go, allowing oneself to be convinced, letting oneself be enchanted [...]." Or, as put in the words of Laruelle, "Consenting at last to the One as to that which keeps the multiplicities beyond Being itself." Scholars such as Alex Galloway and Iain James have been crucial in introducing to the Anglophone world the work of Laruelle who is, in many ways, considered to be among the first of the speculative realists. Laruelle's "non-philosophical thought" is "thought of the multiple and of becoming, of dispersion and of dissemination" and it is at work in the "contemporary hopes of an overflowing [...] Representation" with a "thought of the Absolute [...] a thought of the One, but of the One without unity, beyond the Idea, the Logos, even of Being." Other than Laruelle's own very short and revealing "On the Black Universe: In the Foundations of Human Color" or his more enigmatic *Principles of Non-Philosophy*, Rocco Gangle's *François Laruelle's Philosophies of Difference: A Critical Introduction and Guide* is especially clear as is Alex Galloway's *Laruelle: Against the Digital*. Attempting to summarize Laruelle's (often difficult and quite obscure) thinking the *LA Review of Books* tells us, "For those looking for the next big thing in 'Theory' (critical, philosophical, or otherwise), Laruelle's work can only prove disappointing. He does not aim to improve upon or eclipse that of Derrida, Deleuze, or Badiou (that is, the men of the 1980s, '90s, and '00s, respectively): indeed, to attempt to do so would entirely miss the point of his project. For non-philosophy, the discourse of European 'master-thinkers' is passé. What Laruelle offers us instead is a new way to experience philosophy: neither as the right nor wrong representation of reality (through difference, multiplicity, or eventality, as in Derrida, Deleuze, and Badiou respectively) but as a material, immanent part of it. Laruelle's project of non-philosophy aims at nothing less than a re-vision of what counts as thought, taking it well beyond the hype of philosophical mastery and into a materialism that sees philosophy as only one kind of thinking, one part of what he calls 'the One.'"[2]

Finally, as influenced by the work of Iain Grant, there is a naturalist wing of the post-speculative turn that systematically articulates not in bright or dark tones but generally with indifferent technical precision a philosophy of nature that nevertheless is able to account for nature's generative and dynamic transcendental conditions (drawing upon the technical style of the German idealists but also including an account of sensation or emotion as found in the German romantics). The method of these philosophers in their crafting of a philosophy of nature is "speculative physics" or the "dynamics of the sensible," although conceived from the viewpoint of a *transcendental materialism* (whereas Brassier or Laruelle may be *transcendental realists* first and foremost). However, one must not sell short Brassier's own naturalism for, in this stage of his career he has begun to engage with naturalism and transcendental philosophy alike mostly through the naturalist and process-relational philosophy of Wilfred Sellars and the rationalisms of Plato, Hegel, and Kant. Regardless, this wing at first appears similar to New Materialism and indeed the two overlap, however its emphasis on the idealist tradition, process-relational ontology, and a non-normative form of rationalist philosophy coupled with the complete ontologization of matter, could differentiate the two wings well enough. Additionally, unlike New Materialism the naturalists utilize many of the giants of speculative-systematic philosophy in their *critique* of philosophers such as Bergson or Deleuze (even though they believe they may be asking the right questions). As a speculative naturephilosophy this wing does not focus first and foremost on any self-powering *objects* of nature but is rather concerned with nature's dynamic *transcendental conditions* and *potential*: its *productive grounds* or *powers* anterior to any particular object or material created (therefore creativity rather than created, creation-of-object rather than object-created, *natura naturans* rather than *natura naturata*, *unconscious* rather than *conscious*). The philosophers in this tradition are only "vitalist" in the sense that they are predominantly concerned with nature's ground, powers, location, and movement, albeit without over-privileging the concept of "life" as prior vitalistic traditions have done. Indeed it is the non-reductive, geo-elemental explanation of life-as-conceptual-movement that qualifies any discussion of this naturephilosophy as "neo." Within idealist lines *the* question at stake in this wing is whether transcendental philosophy (location, movement, conditions, source) can be fit with a theoretically adequate and conceptually rigorous form of naturalism. Such a question depends upon the very definition of "naturalism": that there is nothing "other" than nature. Following, *mind* is of a natural history and is natural. And thus many (but not all) of these philosophers adopt some form or version of *panpsychism* or seek to explain consciousness as well as the *unconscious* in ways that are empirical (though not necessarily remaining exclusive of what is immaterial, conceptual, or in some rare cases spiritual). Principal influences include Plato (as a one-world theorist), Schelling, Hegel, Fichte, Kant, Brandom, Peirce, Sellars,

Santayana, and Dewey; and critically Whitehead, Deleuze, and Bergson. More than aesthetical affect or rhetoric like in New Materialism, reason and speculative (abductive) logic or Schellingean intellectual intuition are philosophical means of analysis, as are semiotics and psychoanalysis. Of all the above speculative philosophies it is this wing which is the most "idealist" in its character. Some figures working in this field other than Iain Grant are Didier Debaise (who is also close to New Materialism and has done much to recover and utilize Whiteheadian philosophy), William Connolly (also close to New Materialism, a process-relational philosopher of vital becoming), James R. Williams (a process philosopher of signs), Sean McGrath (who has written on Schelling and the unconscious), Jason Hills (who draws upon non-correlationist, i.e., "speculative" phenomenology as much as he does the naturalism of Dewey and pragmaticism of C.S. Peirce), Leon Niemoczynski (known for his "speculative naturalism" and "bleak theology"), and Robert Corrington (known for his "ecstatic naturalism," a speculative enterprise recognizing nature's unconscious aspect and self-transforming potential, similar to McGrath but also to the "dark vitalists" or "dark materialists").

As it stands the naturephilosophy and neo-rationalist wings of the post-speculative turn in particular appear to be in the most constructive form of dialogue where theoretical cross-over is taking place given several forthcoming texts on the topics of rationality and naturalism, Kant/Brandom/Plato/Sellars, nature and reason in German idealism, assessments of the compatibility between naturalism and transcendental philosophy, and various reassessments of Schelling, Hegel, Kant, and Fichte.

0.4 The New Metaphysics: A Scene Report

Recent events, whether conferences or workshops beyond that of an individual speaker, are only of a few number but nevertheless are important as varying streams of the new metaphysics take shape, evolving and transforming along the way. Beginning in Germany, each year Armen Avanessian of the *Spekulative Poetic* organization runs talks and events where the goal is to connect "the language-based poststructuralist philosophy of recent decades with the contemporary interest in ontology. Speculative thought (be it Hegel's, Benjamin's, or, more recently, Quentin Meillassoux's) calls for a self-determination in its practice of language. In this sense, linguistic and philosophical approaches to language ontology are interested in poiesis, which provide an ontological reinterpretation of the correlationist myth of the world's creation by language: language changes the world." Several workshops have occurred under Armen's direction including the *Speculations on Anonymous Materials* in 2014 (featuring Ray Brassier, Iain Grant, Robin Mackay, and others) and the "Contemporary Materialism, Realism, and Metaphysics" co-organized with Tobias Huber (featuring Meillassoux, Grant, and Brassier) in 2012. (Ray Brassier has on multiple occasions provided lectures in Berlin thanks to this organization.)

Each year in Germany there is a summer school in Bonn which often covers Continental speculative philosophy (billed as a summer school in "German philosophy") although of particular interest would be the third Bonn summer school in 2012 featuring Grant, Brassier, Meillassoux, Hagglund, and Zizek. Papers of these talks are often available online or have been republished as short books or as chapters in books.

Some closely related summer schools held in the Americas include the Pittsburgh Summer Symposium in Contemporary Philosophy, concentrating in 2013 on the work of Schelling (and featuring Iain Grant as a seminar leader), and the Philadelphia Summer School in Contemporary Continental Philosophy (featuring John Caputo leading seminars concentrating on Meillassoux, Brassier, Malabou, and Latour) in 2014. The Philadelphia Entity for Speculative Thought (P.E.S.T.) has also consistently run "underground, off-radar, and off-network" seminars free of charge for those interested in speculative, realist, and materialist philosophy—seminars covering the philosophy of Quentin Meillassoux, Francois Laruelle, Mehdi Belhaj Kacem, and Catherine Malabou, in addition to larger events (such as "Speculative Misanthropy" held in 2014). And nearby in New York the Public School has often run various events featuring contemporary speculative philosophy, where of note would be the series "Dark Nights of the Universe" featuring Galloway, Thacker, and others and Galloway's five night lecture series "French Theory Today" which explored "a new generation of French voices—Catherine Malabou, Bernard Stiegler, Mehdi Belhaj Kacem, Quentin

Meillassoux, and François Laruelle" where, like P.E.S.T., each night consisted of a lecture followed by questions from and discussion with class participants.

In France Louis Morelle reports of the following scholars and their activity, especially the most active of which is the neo-vitalist new metaphysics of nature: Pierre Montebello, who works on what he calls "l'autre métaphysique," by which he means Tarde, Ravaisson, Nietzsche, and Bergson, is very much one important figure in trying to think a metaphysics of nature; as is Frédéric Worms, a specialist of Bergson and contemporary 20th-century French philosophy more generally, under whom an important number of PhD students are now working—especially on Bergson and therefore sometimes on issues related to nature. Meillassoux is obviously instrumental to bringing contemporary metaphysics into view in the last decade followed by Mehdi Belhaj Kacem whose forthcoming book *The Meillassoux Effect* is much anticipated. Olivier Surel, who works on nature and social ontology, is one of the few young people who writes on matters in speculative philosophy along with Quentin Meillassoux and Alain Badiou and has recently published a number of important articles. Morelle also reports that the Simondonians have a journal, *Cahiers Simondon*, which seems to be quite popular in bringing back Deleuzians to their roots in Simondon, but also Tarde and Ruyer (Ruyer's *Neofinalism* was just translated into English and published). Besides Barthelemy (who has written a book on Simondon and nature philosophy), there are Baptiste Morizot Anne Sauvagnargues, and Anne Lefebvre who hold a colloquium called *Cerisy*: http://www.ccic-cerisy.asso.fr/simondon13.html.

Morelle continues that around Didier Debaise and Isabelle Stengers, other Belgian names that regularly turn up are Michel Weber and Vinciane Desprets. They also held a Cerisy colloquium: http://www.ccic-cerisy.asso.fr/gestes13.html. Morelle writes that, "It is noteworthy, I think, that the center of gravity for francophone Whitehead studies is actually outside France."

Morelle tells of the CIEPFC, one of the major places, in Paris, where activity involving the new metaphysics takes place, their members list (http://www.ciepfc.fr/spip.php?rubrique1) points to quite a few interesting names such as Camille Riquier or Ioulia Podoroga, and Patrice Maniglier. (Maniglier participated in the Zagreb conferences on the new metaphysics and materialism, held at the MaMa Multimedia Institute. MaMa also hosted the "To Have Done with Life: Vitalism and Anti-Vitalism" conference in 2011, its third conference featuring Brassier, Hagglund, Malabou, Noys and others; and in 2009 they held the "21st-Century Materialism" conference featuring Peter Hallward and Martin Hagglund. Most recently of note was the "Sophistry: The Powers of the False" conference in 2014 featuring Brassier and Albert Toscano.)

People working on or around Schelling and naturephilosophy, like Alexander Schnell, Miklos Vetö, Xavier Tilliette or Emmanuel Cattin, or Jean-Christope Lemaître are interesting for many. Schnell has recently written a book trying to alter phenomenology in order to make it speculative, *En voie de réel*. And Descola,

Latour, de Castro, and others had a Cerisy colloquium which is worth mention: http://www.ccic-cerisy.asso.fr/metaphysiques13.html. Descola, Latour, and de Castro being among the new generation to appropriate American pragmatism and empiricism as part of their speculative anthropological "multinaturalism." Along those lines Mathias Girel works on James, Peirce, and pragmatism, has read some of Corrington's writing (on nature), and is very fluent in American philosophy in general.

Organized mostly from within France (although also taking place in London) I should mention the *Matter of Contradiction* seminars, held between 2011 and 2014—each year featuring a different theme; so for example the first installment "Art without Aesthetics" in 2011 featured Quentin Meillassoux and Fabien Giraud; the third event held at the Mute Magazine Offices was "War against the Sun" featuring Ray Brassier and Robin Mackay; in 2013 was "Periplum: A Night without Stars" featuring among others Fabien Giraud and Oliver Surel. Also in France PAF (Performing Arts Forum) has been excellent in organizing summer long courses, some of which discuss the new metaphysics (Wolfendale and Land have given presentations in the past). 2016 was its third year.

Sadly I do not have the space to discuss in much further detail the abovementioned exciting developments here as my task is more direct in that I shall try to discuss those most emblematic of the initial speculative turn itself and only at times point toward the developments which have occurred or are occurring thanks to it. But such is the speculative turn in Continental philosophy—new streams and variations are underway. With the information above the reader should have more than enough to go on so as to see who is working on what after the speculative turn.

0.5 A General, Non-Technical Introduction

One final word is in order. I debated as to whether the book should proceed in sections, whether the book should drop into style, whether I should parse out each step of each argument of each philosopher discussed. But it dawned on me that the series to which this book belongs aims to, "provide very short introductions (80–110 pages) written in an accessible style with minimal use of footnotes." So from that statement I discovered what was to become a helpful keyword in buoying the possible (limitless) depth that a book covering the subject of metaphysics might take. From the series' statement that keyword was "accessible." To me, accessibility means a *non-technical*, layperson's style that is clear enough for the general reader to comprehend. It should be informative of course, but it should also be conversational in order to engage the curious. This demands that an epitome, as I see it, be most of all an *informative* but *uncomplicated introduction*. Thus the style (I hope) can be read as simply as possible.

It is with accessibility in mind that my hope also is that this book can be used by undergraduate and perhaps beginning graduate students alike. For a course in Continental philosophy the book perhaps could be used as a book-end, a short encapsulation or epitome of where Continental philosophy stands today in the 21st century and how it got there. This is why I have attempted to show how by taking cue from but three of the most emblematic philosophers of the "speculative turn" we may see how speculative Continental philosophy proceeds "after" it.

It is my hope that, overall, readers will gain from this book an understanding how the evolving motion of concepts created from within the brief life of SR *continues* to change speculative philosophy in the Continental philosophical landscape today, for I believe that the legacy of speculative realism is not that of "Speculative Realism" per se but is of the turn in *spirit* that it helped to initiate. In such spirit I am sure that Continental philosophy will proceed to tackle ever more great, new, and interesting problems. It to those fruitful efforts that I most look forward.

Resources for Further Reading

After Nature blog, "Continental Realism and Materialism: A Guide": http://afterxnature.blogspot.com/p/speculative-realism-guide.html.

Dolphijn, Rick, and Iris van der Tuin, eds., *New Materialism: Interviews & Cartographies* (Michigan: Open Humanities Press, 2012): http://quod.lib.umich.edu/o/ohp/11515701.0001.001.

Ennis, Paul, *Continental Realism* (London: Zero Books, 2011).

Galloway, Alexander, *French Theory Today: An Introduction to Possible Futures*, a pamphlet series documenting the week-long October 2012 seminar at the Public School New York (New

York: TPSNY/Erudio Editions, 2010): http://cultureandcommunication.org/galloway/FTT/French-Theory-Today.pdf.

Gironi, Fabio, "Between Naturalism and Rationalism: A New Realist Landscape," *Journal of Critical Realism* Vol. 11, No. 3 (2015): 361–387: https://www.academia.edu/1501804/Between_Naturalism_and_Rationalism_A_New_Realist_Landscape.

James, Ian, *The New French Philosophy* (London and New York: Polity, 2012).

Niemoczynski, Leon, "21st Century Continental Philosophy: Reflections on Continental Realism and Materialism," *Cosmos & History: The Journal of Natural and Social Philosophy* Vol. 9, No. 2 (2013): 13–31: http://cosmosandhistory.org/index.php/journal/article/viewFile/356/591.

Origgi, Gloria, "What's New About 'New Realism?'" *The Berlin Review of Books* (2016): http://berlinbooks.org/brb/2016/10/whats-new-about-new-realism/.

Notes

1 "Matter Feels, Converses, Suffers, Desires, Yearns and Remembers," interview with Karen Barad, in *New Materialism*, ed. by Dolphijn and Van der Tuin.

2 John Ó Maoilearca, "Galloway's Non-Digital Introduction to Laruelle," *LA Review of Books* (May 17, 2015): https://lareviewofbooks.org/article/galloways-non-digital-introduction-to-laruelle/.

I
Dead on Arrival

1.1 What Is Speculative Realism?

THIS BOOK SEEKS TO ARTICULATE THE MAJOR THEMES, concepts, and ideas present in the thought of several philosophers which best represent within Continental philosophy a renewed interest in *realism*, *materialism*, and *metaphysics* sometimes referred to as "Continental realism and materialism," "new realism," "new materialism," or most generically "the new metaphysics." All of these terms refer to the recent return to an interest in pre-critical, speculative, realist, materialist metaphysics during the beginning of the 21st century. In particular, the philosophies of the French philosopher Quentin Meillassoux and the Scottish-born philosopher Ray Brassier, both of whom participated in a one-day workshop titled "Speculative Realism" (hence this book's title), held at Goldsmith's College, University of London in April of 2007, form the bulk of the book. A third philosopher of equal importance for the development of this recent "speculative turn" (and who also participated in the 2007 "Speculative Realism" workshop), Iain Hamilton Grant and his "transcendental materialism/speculative idealism," serves as a fulcrum position between the "speculative materialism" of Meillassoux and "speculative nihilism/transcendental realism" of Brassier. Explaining the 2007 workshop Brassier writes, "The impetus for the original, eponymous workshop was to revive questions about realism, materialism, science, representation, and objectivity, that were dismissed as otiose by each of the main pillars of Continental orthodoxy: phenomenology, critical theory, and deconstruction."

Given the title of the 2007 workshop and this book, what is speculative realism? And what would a general overview of speculative realism look like? Perhaps a more interesting question might be, what has come *after* speculative realism? As Ben Woodward has described it, speculative realism is the "dead elephant in the room," for there is no such *thing* as "Speculative Realism" proper. There does not appear to be anything substantially philosophically determinate to which we might meaningfully attach the proper name: no concrete school of thought with founding members (what would that school of thought's cohesive essence be? Who are the founding or even current members?), no distinct or common method ("speculation" is simply not specific enough), and no distinguishing feature not common to too many *other* realist, speculative metaphysicians in the history of philosophy so as to render meaningful or informative (and hence warrant) the argument that something like speculative realism "exists" in its own right.

Given that the meaning of speculative realism is quite nebulous yet referenced so often, my goal in this chapter is simply to begin by sketching out what one might *mean* by speculative realism by providing an outline of its *history* (the reader should be warned, this history is by no means pretty). This will, at least in part, help to clarify the sociological-historical referent of the term "speculative realism" as well as distinguish that referent from philosophically defensible extant trends independent of it. This will also help to articulate the difference between the turn to 21st-century speculative philosophy, i.e., "the new metaphysics" or "Continental realism and materialism" from any so-called Speculative Realist "movement." Of this so-called "movement," Ray Brassier, who coined the term "Speculative Realism," explains in rather straightforward but ruthlessly honest terms:

> The "speculative realist movement" exists only in the imaginations of a group of bloggers promoting an agenda for which I have no sympathy whatsoever: actor-network theory spiced with pan-psychist metaphysics and morsels of process philosophy. I don't believe the internet is an appropriate medium for serious philosophical debate; nor do I believe it is acceptable to try to concoct a philosophical movement online by using blogs to exploit the misguided enthusiasm of impressionable

> graduate students. I agree with Deleuze's remark that ultimately the most basic task of philosophy is to impede stupidity, so I see little philosophical merit in a "movement" whose most signal achievement thus far is to have generated an online orgy of stupidity.

Here Brassier refers to the flurry of online activity (mostly deplorable and which lasted several years, generating exceptional animosity through multiple blogs, the main venue through which those interested in the subject would engage with others); this, which followed the 2007 workshop and the eventual "selling out" and "branding" of the promise that desired to approach Continental philosophy differently, that is pre-critically and speculatively, as well as the eventual recognition of a sort of "death" of speculative realism as the online flurry surrounding the after-effects of the workshop eventually died out. A short history of this online activity is described in a telling blog post "On Speculative Realism and Circular Firing Squads," where the comments section reveals more than the initial post itself, found here: http://drjon.typepad.com/jon_cogburns_blog/2014/10/on-speculative-realism-and-circular-firing-squads.html.

As one is able to tell from the comments section to the above blog post, we learn from Robin Mackay, editor of *Collapse*, the very journal which published the Speculative Realism workshop transcripts (which we are told he now bitterly regrets), as to what "really happened" during these years (2007 until roughly 2012–13 at the latest, with 2011 being a "peak"), specifically with respect to how, through blog discussion, philosophical innovation and debate was stymied by a disturbingly common trend of vile, personal attacks directed to those who were attempting to enter into the discussion.

In short, a sort of factionalist "gang mentality" arose where through a sustained several-years-long flame war various factions battled each other online with the goal of staking a flag in the ground regarding *who* would determine the meaning of "Speculative Realism" or belong to its "ranks." These factional skirmishes—to put it rather mildly—were not without their very real and personal dangers however. As Robin Mackay explains, "[T]hings got worse. [There were] vile personal attacks on friends and associates, concentrating not only on their academic 'failure' (somehow seen to be the worst sin and to warrant dismissal of anything they may say) but also their character, motives, and even their mental health (the worst of these have now been removed [...] at the very strong request of others, but they are on record elsewhere)."

The methods of attack and career assassination were underhanded. Some individuals were simply ignored and intentionally left out of the discussion so that their work disappeared into the black hole of unacknowledgement, their careers faltering as a result. Others were subjected to online ridicule and harassment which bled into personal interactions behind closed doors as specific individuals were blackballed with negative comments "in passing." Still others became targets of quite vile and personally directed attacks in that outright smear campaigns took place seeking to take-down and relegate as unimportant anyone who *dared* challenge a claim as to what speculative realism was about. To make matters worse, so-called "pile-ons" in the comments sections of blogs were not the exception, they were the rule. The promise of blogs to host enlightened reasonable discussion quickly developed into the practice of philosophy-as-blood sport and yellow philosophical journalism. Each ideologically aligned faction would employ a selective-awareness bubble by ignoring the other before virulently lashing out so as to inflict the most damage. Ownership over the meaning of "Speculative Realism" engendered some of the most reprehensible online behavior that one could possibly observe. Those who were called out on such behavior smugly responded that how they behaved online in no way represented how they behaved "in person." Still, the effects of the bad online behavior were very real for those affected by it, and "Speculative Realism" became synonymous with an "online orgy of stupidity."

That said, it is ironic that the "best" of speculative realism actually came in the form of online criticisms *of* it. In particular, the thinking of Terence Blake, Jason Hills, and Pete Wolfendale. These philosophers were, strangely, ignored despite their gargantuan efforts of criticizing with impeccable *argument* (rather than uncouth rhetorical affect) some speculative realist faction or another, each quite independently calling out charlatanism and house-of-cards philosophies where they saw them. Even to this day Jason Hill's blog *Immanent Transcendence*—which is no longer active—is a goldmine of incisive arguments concerning factional Speculative Realism, as is the blog of Terence Blake *Agent Swarm* and the blog of Pete

Wolfendale, *Deontologistics*. Yet the criticisms of Blake, Hills, and Wolfendale have until this day been met with a repugnant silence despite the adequacy of their criticism. The fact that in many cases their arguments made their way past blogs through to peer-reviewed publication makes such silence all the more "weird."

If questioned whether there is solidly a new "school" or "movement" of something called Speculative Realism, something other than the blemish of regrettable online history to which the *name* "Speculative Realism" might refer, the answer is quite simply, "no." However, this is not to say that within Continental philosophy a speculative turn did not take place nor that it cannot be said that the recent return to realism, materialism, and metaphysics might not collectively (and for the sake of convenience) be referenced as "the new metaphysics" or "Continental realism and materialism." But even this convenient grouping does pose its challenges. For example, some might claim that an "essence" of speculative realism might be in some common call to oppose "correlationism" (the view that the world cannot be thought independently of the being thinking about it). But at times even this seems to be too strong as not all contemporary speculative, realist philosophers accept the call to oppose that view. It seems impossible therefore to account for speculative realism to be any kind of existing *movement* despite some vague intellectual affinity in discussing correlationism or beginning from that point. As Wolfendale explains, "The only thing that could possibly bind SR together as a coherent intellectual movement was Meillassoux's intellectual call to arms in the fight against correlationism,

[and] it has become increasingly apparent that [...] we are indeed at war with this pervasive epistemological scepticism that metastasised across the humanities in the latter half of the twentieth century." Yet as Wolfendale then goes on to acknowledge, and Brassier reaffirm, this has nothing whatsoever to do with any name-branded Speculative ®ealism™ if in fact *specific claims are made upon some concrete or definite nature that warrants a proper name let alone "brand" or "movement."* It therefore seems that speculative and realist philosophy, in following Meillassoux's call to embrace the openness of speculative thinking and reject the kind of finitude associated with dogmatism, might only suggest *a style of the times* rather than indefatigably lay claim over some name-brand or concrete movement. And as this style is broadly generic, it seems that no one specific name can attach to it.

1.2 A Review of the Literature and a Short History of Speculative Realism

Regarding the proper name "Speculative Realism," then, upon analysis it refers to nothing more than a 2007 one-day workshop where for the first time the metaphysical break with traditional Continental philosophy was made transparent. Given this, it seems more appropriate to describe the new metaphysics under discussion here, simply as 21st-century speculative philosophy or a new metaphysics, realist and materialist in orientation, in order to preserve the non-dogmatic and open impetus called for by Meillassoux in his definition of metaphysics-as-speculation—this so as to avoid freezing with premature and false borders an impetus which dares to move from Kantian finitude (influencing phenomenology, existentialism, hermeneutics, post-structuralism, deconstruction, or "postmodernism" generally) to a still moving and developing constellation of ideas found in the axis of *realism*, *materialism*, and *metaphysics*, all re-imagined yet taking cue from key historical moments (French rationalism, German idealism, ancient Greek materialism, American pragmatism, and Sellarsian naturalism, etc.).

It must be stated that Meillassoux, Brassier, or Grant *do not* self-identify as "speculative realists" and all disavow the label as impugning a false cohesion among them other than their being present at the 2007 workshop. As Meillassoux has described, "Speculative Realism is an appellation designating in itself nothing important but with which I have become associated. It does not quite correspond to my enterprise since it also comprises the option that I seek to counter." For as radical as the 2007 workshop was in making transparent this renewed interest in Continental realism and materialism and as it served to be a historical marking point for a sign of the times, a certain effort took place to co-opt and "brand" this interest. Many believed that through this branding any promise for the initial impetus of the speculative turn was "sold out." Given the lack of common index discussed a moment ago, yet the claim upon the 2007 workshop's spirit as a "brand," speculative realism proper was claimed rather infamously to be "dead on arrival." In other words, nothing like a proper Speculative Realism existed—but immediately the initial promise of the 2007 workshop was staked and claimed through the identification of a movement-as-brand: that of Speculative ®ealism™. As Pete Wolfendale explains,

> The claim that SR doesn't exist is simply the claim that there isn't any distinctive philosophical common ground indexed [...] However, this is entirely compatible with the claim that at one point it looked like there might be, and that this promised a potentially new philosophical trajectory that would be genuinely distinct from extant trends. The sense in which SR can be said to have "died" is simply the sense in which this promise proved to be false.

The open sense of speculation identified by Meillassoux and the promise of speculative realism did not continue after the one-day workshop. For ten years I have been a commentator on the development of the philosophies under discussion in this book, and I have seen firsthand several transformations take place that confirm the following observations which suggest that inevitably speculative realism was "stillborn" or born dead, prematurely petrified, or perhaps never existed at all save for a falsified promise—and the claim to some sort of name brand Speculative ®ealism™ has done nothing except to *exclude* scholars active in the field of Continental metaphysics by determining a "we" or "us" membership. A simple search online reveals the dynamics and power-plays of this name-branding effort, and the interactions and comments on the blogs which originally propagated the promise of speculative realism reveal exactly what Ray Brassier, in his "Speculative Autopsy" reports. Without trawling through comment sections in blogs looking for grievances and going by memory only, my general impression of that activity during the years of 2007 until roughly 2012–13 (2011 being a "peak") was one of moral outrage, if not disgust.

Eventually discussion smoldered and died out as the senselessness of "debate" concerning speculative realism became apparent, for the positions in play *had no justification*. One finds mere assertion, rhetorical flourish and marketing, but no substantive argument. And so Brassier turned out to be correct. Blogs initially lit the tinder of the new metaphysics, however due to the intrinsic nature of attempting to engage philosophy online and the pitfalls that come with it, there was a flash in the pan and things faded as quickly as they came on.

But what of any scholarship concerning "Speculative Realism?" In the nearly ten years since the original 2007 workshop just two books that are commentaries on speculative realism with the proper name in their title have appeared. Both unfortunately bowdlerize their content by offering some very odd choices for representatives of the so-called "speculative realist" movement yet exclude some of the most active voices of appraisal. (Again, there is no mention of Blake, Hills, and Wolfendale despite the numerous publications written among them—publications that not only contributed to the conversation, but in fact steered the very *meaning* of that conversation). Further, contemporary philosophers who *could* be said to be offering speculative and realist metaphysics, namely Francois Laruelle or perhaps even Catherine Malabou, were curiously absent. Is this because the proper name of Speculative Realism refers only to something quite arbitrary, or for other reasons? One may never know.

A third book (which does not have "Speculative Realism" in its title, thankfully titling the speculative turn simply as "the new realism," pronounces an end of phenomenology in the name of branded Speculative ®ealism™ but then falls flat as it turns out that the end described is not the end of phenomenology but that of Speculative Realism itself. Dan Zahavi's "The End of What? Phenomenology vs. Speculative Realism" details this book's contradictory conclusion which is either phenomenology does not exist or never began, however this seems also to apply to *speculative realism itself*. Again, the motivation here seems to be the validation of an existence claim regarding "Speculative Realism" by arguing for the *non-existence* of phenomenology. Whether there is SR or trying to find out who is SR seems to be more important than any substantive explication of the new realism. As with the other two books only close allies seem to be included at the expense of excluding some of the most up-to-the-moment critical appraisals of, or contemporary developments within, Continental speculative thinking.

With the failure of Speculative ®ealism™ in mind Brassier's "Speculative Autopsy" demonstrates as fact that while some may *talk* about speculative realism that does not mean that there is a substantive or existing "movement" beneath the thin veneer of a brand Speculative ®ealism™, despite whatever attempts there are to capture, control, and profit from branding its meaning. Name-branding is dangerous because it claims as exclusive specific ground by excluding those who either challenge the validity of that ground or have in fact claimed their own in the realist spirit (through publication, by blog, etc.). And so the end result turns out not to be any true speculative realism, but a specious branded realism. Again, Wolfendale elaborates:

> [Branded SR] has diluted Speculative Realism until nothing is left but Specious Realism, and thereby destroyed any promise that the original grouping [the 2007 workshop] might have had.

And,

> Those who enthusiastically leapt into the melee, enthused by the renewal that SR seemed to promise, have found themselves at once unwillingly conscripted into a dubious "movement" promoted by an efficiently-organized PR operation, and continually reprimanded for stepping out of line (a "neurology death cult" charged with "continental scientism", "reductionism", and more besides). We must refuse to march under a banner that has been co-opted as a means to suppress rather than

to stimulate thinking; and we must admit: Speculative Realism was dead on arrival.

The "death" of speculative realism, its being "dead on arrival," or its "meltdown" (described by Nick Land) consists in those involved in this speculative turn coming to a consensus that the branding of the name speculative realism in essence *forecloses* any flexible promise of the openness of speculation.

Over the years the spirit of speculation was centered in the initial position that Continental philosophy had taken the wrong path when given the decision to follow Kant critically or Hegel speculatively. But any common ground ends there: reject Kantian finitude and embrace the Hegelian speculative moment. Beyond that initial move, no name could capture a cohesive essence of the sheer multiplicity of positions taking up that Hegelian sleeping giant. In the language of Derrida and Hegel, naming of this sort is a magical capture and murder.

1.3 Why Discuss Speculative Realism?

Given all of the above, the telling of the history of speculative realism certainly may leave a sour taste in one's mouth. And of course one may ask at this point, if speculative realism was "dead on arrival" (pace Brassier's "Speculative Autopsy" postscript written for Wolfendale's latest which is, as it has been said, "one long obituary for speculative realism") then why talk about it? Why bother with such a tired debate over a mere label? Why discuss speculation, realism, or materialism in any conjoined sense? Let me attempt to turn to a more positive account of the tale in order to glean what we might learn from it. In this more positive account I shall attempt to focus on the *ideas* in question rather than the *histrionics*.

First, "speculation" here means, according to Meillassoux, not dogmatically claiming *what is* (pace traditional dogmatic metaphysics) but articulating what *can be*. According to Meillassoux, speculation benefits from a metaphysics "not of *substance* or of *closed system*, but of the Open (Bergson), of the event (Whitehead), of singularity-in-becoming (Simondon)."[1] Speculation is therefore not *limited* by the finite categories of the human understanding, by the experience of human consciousness, by interpretation of text or sign, or by the social construction and power-legislation of discursive formation, all staples of Continental philosophy until the occurrence of the speculative turn. Indeed, speculation is freed in all of its radical contingency "outside of the text," to focus pre-critically on an absolute reality itself, a "great Outdoors" lost previously to Continental thought from Kant right through to Husserl, Heidegger, Sartre, Ponty, Foucault, and Derrida. Indeed, I am of the opinion that Meillassoux's *After Finitude* and his challenge to the orthodoxy of standard opinion in Continental thought warrants considerable attention. In a more general sense, Meillassoux has *challenged us to follow the path of speculation rather than criticism or dogmatism*.

Second, we must speak of *realism* and *materialism*, in addition to metaphysics-as-speculation, if we are to heed Meillassoux's call. The realism under discussion here is neither dogmatically robust, as in Plato, nor skeptically naive, as in Anglo-American analytical philosophy. The speculation in question frees the real to present its *own* possibilities and events, its *own* nature, without being dependent upon the human being or human ideas for its constitution. Regardless of name, the result is the same: Realism and materialism are re-conceived not only because reality is acknowledged to be quite independent of human subjectivity (Brassier's speculative nihilism and transcendental realism), in its most radical extreme reality is claimed to be in-itself devoid of subjectivity (Meillassoux's speculative materialism). And while Meillassoux, Brassier, and Grant diverge on the details of this idea the general milieu is the same: the human is thought to no longer occupy the center of reality and reality can be known independent of any specific human contribution to it—both long-time staple dictums of Continental philosophy traditionally conceived. True, *many* contemporary philosophers have taken this direction—however in my judgment, when positioning the radically different philosophies of Meillassoux, Grant, and Brassier in conversation, penetration into the nature of the practice of metaphysical philosophy appears to yield important insight. There appears to be a reactivation of objectivity, of philosophy's relationship to the natural sciences, to physics and cosmology, mathematics, and most of all, to *rationality*. Thus, a return to realism albeit modified; a return to materialism albeit modified; all under the umbrella of speculative philosophy.

Other than Meillassoux, Brassier, and Grant, of course there are others who pre-date this speculative turn and whose philosophy is all of speculative, materialist, and realist (modifying the exact meaning of these terms as Meillassoux, Brassier, and Grant all do). For example, it is quite possible to say that philosophers such as Gilles Deleuze swam against the 20th-century Continental current of anti-realist and anti-metaphysical philosophy in his writing of *Difference and Repetition*. Alfred North Whitehead, partially an American philosopher but important for influencing some Continental thinkers, as well could be claimed to have a speculative and realist philosophy. Today, in France Francois Laruelle could enter into the discussion as could Mehdi Belhaj Kacem, Bruno Latour, Isabelle Stengers, or many others.

In a positive sense the constellation of realism, materialism, and metaphysics has surpassed the late 20th-century "theological turn" as a speculative one, where contemporary Continental thought has taken a step back to follow the path of Hegel's speculative thinking, deal in some manner with correlationist thinking, and re-assess what occurs when one follows Kant, as 20th-century Continental philosophy did. Such a turn from Kant to Hegel in fact *was* a real occurrence. As it stands today this is evidenced by a renewed interest in Hegel and the German idealists, indeed an interest in German *Naturphilosophie* most generally. Following to some degree Badiou, Continental philosophers are reevaluating the speculative tools of mathematics and set-theory as well in order to reach ontological and cosmological conclusions (recently Badiou has commented upon his interest in, and the influence upon him of, the American speculative metaphysician and pragmatist C.S. Peirce). In that sense the natural sciences and power of mathematics, *mathesis*, is no longer seen as foe but as speculative tool (this was foreshadowed in the work of Badiou and his debt to Plato, set-theory, and mathematical philosophy). And finally there is a reassessment of the role of the sciences proper in Continental philosophy, most notably neuroscience and neurobiology, as found in the work of Catherine Malabou, which has ushered in the embrace of a new sort of materialism—one that is not blank and mechanical but rather self-powering and independent of human-read traits. In the same breath we therefore could also mention some of the philosophers mentioned in Ian James' *The New French Philosophy* including Bernard Stiegler, Jacques Ranciere, and Alain Badiou, all of whom to some degree or another repitch how we ought to conceive of the material vis-à-vis the real. Christopher Watkin's *French Philosophy Today: New Figures of the Human in Badiou, Meillassoux, Malabou, Serres, and Latour* offers an introductory account to the spirit of the new metaphysics, as does Alexander Galloways' *The New Realists*. One could easily also turn to the anthology *The Speculative Turn: Continental Realism and Materialism* or Paul Ennis' *Continental Realism*, Lee Braver's *A Thing of This World: A History of Continental Anti-Realism*, Malik and Avenessian's *Genealogies of Speculation*, or the dated (and hence clairvoyant) *Speculative Philosophy* by Andrew Reck (my personal suggestion for a first-read in order to gain bearing on Continental metaphysics and its history). All of these texts and philosophers just mentioned have played a part in the still-ongoing, still developing motion of the constellation of realism, materialism, and metaphysics and the de-centering of the human subject in favor of the real in-itself: in short, *the abandonment of Kantian finitude* and speculative turn toward realist-materialist metaphysics.

1.4 Reading the Rites of Burial

To conclude, it is for these reasons I prefer to speak of the new metaphysics or 21st-century speculative philosophy as Continental realism and materialism, the "new metaphysics," rather than any co-opted name brand. And again, I prefer not to speak of Speculative ®ealism™ but only of the thought of three emblematic thinkers who offer varying and brilliant ways to challenge the orthodoxies of Continental philosophy—this in the key of pre-critical speculative philosophy which resists dogmatism and refashions both realism and materialism. To accomplish this goal, the majority of this book centers on the new metaphysics' confrontation with Kantian finitude, or the idea that transcendental conditions of human subjectivity prohibit claims about what is real before proceeding on to discuss the general tendency of 20th-century Continental philosophy to see the real as saturated with some element of subjectivity. To that end the majority of the book focuses on Quentin Meillassoux and his confrontation in *After Finitude* with the post-Kantian metaphysical heritage of Continental philosophy. Toward the close of the book I discuss how Brassier and Grant both extend and ramify this confrontation within the domains of naturalism, but each with their own twist (Sellarsian and Schellingean naturalism respectively).

With this procedure I hope not to point to any ultimate form of cohesiveness in all three's confrontation with correlationism but to identify their mutual concern with speculative, realist, materialist metaphysics.

As Ray Brassier has said, Speculative Realism is "vitiated by its fatal lack of cohesiveness. Whether we try to define it negatively by what it is against or positively by what it is for, we exclude too little and include too much [...] In the absence of even a minimal positive criterion of doctrinal cohesiveness, all that is left is chatter about something called 'Speculative Realism.'"[2] I am also in agreement with Brassier when he writes, "Is there anything of real philosophical importance at stake in the controversy over what Meillassoux calls 'correlationism'? I think that there is indeed, but unfortunately this is what has been obscured by the concerted attempt to brand."[3] But, also, through the mining of new conceptual possibilities "it does seem possible to reignite a breakout." This entails "rearticulating the questions that the Speculative Realism workshop had initially promised to take up."[4]

If Wolfendale's book is the obituary of speculative realism, and Brassier's postscript its autopsy, then here in this book *we read the rites of burial*. Although this burial is not one of mourning, but of celebration, for from within the Meillassouxian Open we finally walk *after* speculative realism into the next chapter of the new metaphysics and Continental speculative philosophy. It is with cue from the likes of Grant, Brassier, and Meillassoux then that this mantle may be taken up and speculative metaphysics continue to go forward to break past the frenzy which blocked the road of inquiry concerning the future of speculative philosophy. Indeed in the post-contemporary condition "the past is over" and the future of Continental philosophy "after" the so-called speculative turn has only just begun.

Resources for Further Reading

Agent Swarm blog: https://terenceblake.wordpress.com/.

Brassier, Ray, interviewed by Marcin Rychter, "I Am a Nihilist Because I Still Believe in Truth." *Kronos* March 4, 2011: http://kronos.org.pl/?23151,896.

Brassier, Ray, "Postscript: Speculative Autopsy," in Peter Wolfendale, *The Noumenon's New Clothes* (Falmouth: Urbanomic, 2014).

Brassier, Ray, interviewed by Leon Niemoczynski, "Ray Brassier Interview with After Nature Blog," *After Nature* (August 8, 2012): http://afterxnature.blogspot.com/2012/08/ray-brassier-interviews-with-after_26.html.

Deontologistics blog: https://deontologistics.wordpress.com/.

Immanent Trancendence blog: http://immanenttranscedence.blogspot.com/.

Mackay, Robin, ed., *Collapse Vol. II: Speculative Realism* (Falmouth: Urbanomic, 2007).

Mackay, Robin, "Video Lecture Series on Speculative Realism," *DOCH Stockholm University of the Arts* (2011): https://vimeo.com/29879730.

"Why Is Speculative Realism?" ect podcast (June 8, 2016): https://ectpodcast.wordpress.com/2016/06/08/ect-6-why-speculative-realism/.

Notes

1. Interview with Quentin Meillassoux, *Influences* (February 5, 2010): http://www.lesinfluences.fr/2-Que-peut-dire-la-metaphysique.html.
2. Brassier/Wolfendale, "Postscript: Speculative Autopsy," 416.
3. Brassier/Wolfendale, "Postscript: Speculative Autopsy," 421.
4. Brassier/Wolfendale, "Postscript: Speculative Autopsy," 421.

II
Heirs of Kantian Finitude

2.1 The Subject at Center

THE PURPOSE OF THIS CHAPTER IS TO INTRODUCE TO the reader in very general historical terms what speculative realist and materialist philosophy has identified as "correlationism" (this will be further elaborated upon in the subsequent chapter that specifically covers the work of Quentin Meillassoux, however in this chapter I limit my discussion of the concept to its historical articulations). Correlationism as a historical moment finds its apex in the philosophies of Kant and Nietzsche. Kant and Nietzsche both created a subject-at-center metaphysics that has shaped the development of Continental philosophy's approach to realism—where this approach has been dominant until present day despite its critique as offered by the speculative realist and materialist philosophers who are discussed in this book (Quentin Meillassoux, Iain Grant, and Ray Brassier). The chapter is divided into metaphysics before Kant and metaphysics after Kant, with Nietzsche's philosophy identified as a particularly interesting turning point in the appropriation of Kantian subject-at-center philosophy.

As we know, the theme of discussion so far is how in the 21st century there has been a resurgence of *realism*, *materialism*, and *metaphysics*, i.e., *the speculative turn*. This resurgence could be argued to have radically changed the landscape of Continental philosophy as we know it, including Continental philosophy's theoretical trajectories, aims, principal goals of anti-realist deconstruction and subject-at-center phenomenological metaphysics. More broadly stated however, by "Continental philosophy" I simply refer to the post-transcendental, phenomenological, existential, hermeneutic, post-structuralist, and deconstructive philosophies of the 20th century found predominantly in Europe, whether Germany, France, or elsewhere. Major figures representative of the post-Kantian tradition could include Edmund Husserl, Martin Heidegger, Jean-Paul Sartre, Hans-Georg Gadamer, Michelle Foucault, and Jacques Derrida to name just a few.

If one were to venture a hallmark of Continental philosophy as practiced in the 20th century, it may look something like follows. The postmodern Continental tradition has had its theoretical framework defined by its placing of the subject at the center of its ontology, thereby rendering fundamentally epistemological, and in turn normative, anything initially to claimed to be in-itself metaphysical. If we look for the root of this type of thinking we may say it could be found earliest in the 20th century (1900, the death of Nietzsche) in the subsequent reception of Nietzsche's writings. Yet while Nietzsche utilized subject-at-center ontology he did not invent it. Going back further still to the modern period we may state the subject-at-center starting point for all of theoretical inquiry may be traced back through Immanuel Kant to the thinking of Rene Descartes. It was Descartes after all who pursued the much sought after *certainty* of the subject, required so that the sciences could continue to go forward in Enlightenment progress. A champion of reason and methodological skepticism, Descartes invoked doubt so as to retain the only thing which could not be doubted away: the very *fact* of his doubting. In this fact was to be found the activity of thought. There cannot be such an activity without a subject to enact the activity. Thinking, doubting, affirming, judging, denying were acts of what Descartes claimed was most certain of all: the *res cogitans* or "thinking thing." But how did Descartes' placement of the subject at the center of ontology, prior to Nietzsche, then *delimit* metaphysical inquiry so that when Nietzsche found the *cogito* its standpoint was *relative*, *ephemeral*, and *perspectival*? This question can be resolved by turning to the champion of modern philosophy, Immanuel Kant, for it is he who marks the great initiation of what Meillassoux has titled, "The Era of Correlation."

Like Descartes, Kant, too, sought after the certain conditions of human knowledge, albeit in a different way. He transcendentally deduced through the isolation of the categories of the human understanding the required and indeed *necessary* conditions for any possible knowledge. As Alain Badiou tells us in the Preface to Meillassoux's *After Finitude*, "Kant upholds the necessity of the laws of nature [...] concluding that since this necessity cannot have arisen from our sensible receptivity, it must have source: that of the constituting activity of a universal subject, which Kant calls 'the transcendental subject.'"[1] Thus for Kant, subjectivity is transcendentally anchored in a priori conditions of our understanding. It becomes evident how easy a transition can be made from Kant through to a subject-oriented ontology that is less about reality itself or existence qua existence than it is about the place of the subject in the world, the subject's phenomenological *experience*.

According to Lee Braver in his book, *A Thing of this World: A History of Continental Anti-Realism*, within Immanuel Kant's transcendental idealism, which in some ways is very much a continuation of the Cartesian quest for certainty, there begins a motion *toward a radical kind of ontological finitude*. According to Braver, along with this motion toward ontological finitude comes a general *anti-realist* trend which remains a driving force behind postmodern thinking. And indeed, according to Brassier, Grant, and Meillassoux, there are many lines of thought which extend directly from Kant to postmodernist philosophy, and hence directly to anti-realism.

The strongest of these ties happens to be what Meillassoux titles "correlationism." A fuller treatment of correlationism can be found in later chapters of this book, however for now it should suffice to define it as "the idea according to which we only ever have access to the correlation between thinking and being, and never to either term considered apart from the other."[2] Or, perhaps even more clearly, "'Correlationism' [...] [is the view that] there are no objects, no events, no laws, no beings which are not always-already correlated with a point of view, with a subjective access."[3] Therefore correlationist philosophy would include transcendental philosophy, the various kinds phenomenology (existential phenomenology, etc.), existentialism, hermeneutics, post-structuralism, deconstruction, and virtually all of postmodernism.

The correlationist viewpoint is one in which it is assumed that one cannot un-problematically think of or speak of a world that is completely independent of speech or thought. The perspective is *finite* because it is constrained by the necessary conditions (or perspective) which make knowing possible. Yet to say one "knows" in this case is only to say that one knows the world "as" X. If X is reality then reality is always already X-as. So a correlationist is anyone who denies that thought cannot think "the unthought" (that is, X alone; the world *without us*). For the correlationist, "knowledge of a reality [absolutely] *independent* of thought is untenable," the result of which is "a subtle form of idealism that is nonetheless almost ubiquitous."[4] Unlike the speculative realist, the correlationist cannot *non-inferentially* "commerce with reality in-itself through-itself."[5] And so at once we can see that any confrontation of the correlationist view must at the very least involve its proposed alternatives: *realism* to the correlationist's *anti-realism*, and *materialism* to the correlationist's *subjective* or *transcendental idealism*.

In order to avoid the risk of unfairly caricaturizing Kant and fall prey to the error that "in order to be a speculative realist one must *refute* correlationism," I must pay Kant his due. This means that we must engage the Kantian critical system of metaphysics (conceived as an a priori science) in its own terms before placing it in the context of Meillassoux's critique of correlationism. This will determine—as subtle as they might be—how and in what ways the Kantian critical system indeed limits our purchase upon reality in the way that the new realists claim that it does. In order to accomplish this we first must identify Kant's central motive and goal and explain how the ontological problem he deals with was bestowed upon him by his medieval and ancient Greek predecessors. Now, in this text I can only embark upon a *brief* characterization of this history, but in doing so we at least have engaged Kant on his own terms. Only then may we turn toward the specifics of the new metaphysics in its confrontation with correlationism to see how its claim that a correlation between thought and being is necessary ties directly back to the thinking of Kant.

2.2 Metaphysics before Kant

Our story begins with a simple conceptual union made by the ancient Greek pre-Socratic philosopher, Parmenides. The union he made was so elemental that in many respects the history of philosophy can be said to begin with him (rather than Thales, or arguably in other ways Socrates). And, of course, as Meillassoux puts it, "the Parmenidean postulate, 'being and thinking are the same,' remained the prescription for all philosophy up to and including Kant."[6]

It was from the Parmenidean claim that *thought* and *being* are the same that the very *logos* of philosophical thinking would be determined: the law of identity, the law of excluded middle, and the basic law of non-contradiction. This *logos* rests not only on the identification of being-as-thought but that *there can be no non-being*. If all is being-thought (as there cannot be non-being, so whatever is and nothing is not), and if being and thought beyond appearances are truly one, then the *All is One*.

There are two consequences which follow from this. First, reality is necessarily a One, but it is also an *immobile* One. Mobility (and any contingency required for things to be otherwise than what they are) requires non-being in order for one event to follow another event or for one event (or being) to differ from any other; which is to say that if All is One then there cannot be separate events or identities, and further, without change there cannot be distinct *time*. If All is One then the One is *eternity*. Secondly, and as we shall see, Meillassoux finds it *more* problematic how the Parmenidean *logos* nevertheless collapses being *into* thought. Not only is the One of necessity (there is no change, no virtual nature present within it), its ontological character is *thought*, thought becomes a *spiritualized logos*.

It should be noted that a few lines later in *After Finitude* Meillassoux softens his view of the Parmenidean logos, claiming that keeping thought and being *distinct* and *opposed* is the worse of the two mistakes. Meillassoux claims that it is more dangerous to think that there cannot be thought without being, nor being without thought, than it is to speak of a One. In this Meillassoux hints that Parmenides should be commended despite the One taking up being into thought in its monist, spiritualized plane. As well, one might see an affinity here between all of Hegel, Meillassoux, and Laruelle in taking the One as all-things-being equal "in-One"—in a kind of deep ancestral ontological facticity.

The division of a One, the singular real, into a "two" of being which maintains a correlation of being and thought, is found in Plato. For Plato, there is a sense in which being—that is *real Being*—is of an intelligible nature and is *not of this world*. For Plato, the intelligible and truly real cannot change; it is necessary and thus itself *eternal*. Moreover, the intelligible, like in Parmenides, is spiritualized in the sense that the *activity of* thought, for Plato "soul," is part and parcel of the immaterial realm of Being despite the soul's housing in a material body.

Immediately we can see that rather than thought and being collapsing into One they are kept distinct and opposite. So for example Platonic spirit is *not* sensible matter, and so on. Still we might say that the sensible world of matter and intelligible realm of spirit are "always-already" co-related given the fact that the soul, or intellect, embodied in *this* world, *depends upon* an immobile spiritual plane for its origination and eventual return upon death. The material of soul, spirit, is itself eternal and thereby serves as a mediating connection point between sensible matter and intelligible world of Being. And so the question arises: for Plato, do thought and being always already come paired? May one have thought without being or being without thought in Platonic metaphysics?

On the standard interpretation, for Plato, reality is divided into the sensible, phenomenal world of appearances—a world of becoming, change, and imperfection. Intelligible universals or Ideals or Forms are standards of perfection which are substantially eternal in themselves. In other words, the Forms are endowed with *necessity*. This spiritual or immaterial realm of perfection and eternity, Plato tells us, is Being itself. To achieve real being within the gradualist scale of non-Being to full-Being is the aim and goal of all of creation. Through being kept distinct the physical, material world can only be a copy or pale reflection of true Being. The spiritual authority of Being is simply its ontological facticity: *eternal certitude*.

Note however how this standard interpretation is very different than the interpretation constructed by the new metaphysics—especially within the work of Iain Hamilton Grant. Grant, who, in a very radical move, identifies Plato *as a one-world theorist* and locates the veracity of the Idea (the Platonic Form) *within nature* rather than in a realm other to it. This is important to note because the two-world theorist interpretation was and still is essentially *the* interpretation of Platonic metaphysics (even by Kant himself who employed the phenomenal—noumenal distinction). But like, for example, Brassier's unique reconstruction of Kant or Bergson, where conceptual activity is thoroughly naturalized (conceptual activity is natural although nature is not completely conceptual), Grant, likewise, *naturalizes Platonic metaphysics*. Grant writes, "In addition to overhauling the concepts of nature, becoming and being, Platonism is also a contemporary problem, lying at the heart of philosophy becoming capable once again of metaphysics [...] [that] metaphysics cannot be pursued independently of physics [...] The very idea of a Platonic physics removes the ground from the self-conception of post-Nietzschean philosophy's constant inversions of Platonism; it follows, however, from that physics that it is these very inversions that create the two-worlds metaphysics that made them necessary in the first place."[7]

If Plato's metaphysics and its doctrine of substantial forms upholds the correlation between thought and being, between natural and supernatural, between sensible and intelligible, and if each one term within any correlated pair is somehow "beyond" nature yet in contact with it, the burden lies upon how one is to *know* the truth or eternal veracity of those Forms. Of course, for Plato, it was the soul (especially the souls of Philosopher Kings) that is best able to "divine" this spiritual or intelligible world of what we shall identify as "Truth," essential certitude. Thus through spiritual recollection and internal intuition the soul finds its way back to its home (a tale told in Plato's *Phaedrus* where the soul is likened to a magnet attracted to what is most like itself in nature). The story is one of *exitus reditus*.

Plato's ultimate form was that of "the Good." The Good encompassed all of truth (wisdom), beauty, goodness, and justice; the "transcendentals" of medieval philosophy. As an objective determinant the Good was the ultimate ideal object toward which all of creation strives, and indeed by which all of creation can be judged in its normative worth.

This ultimately true, good, just, and beautiful form was interpreted by medieval philosophers to be God: *onto-theologically* God as *first cause* and most *supreme being*. And in modern philosophy, the rationalists maintained that God is an ultimate form of spiritual truth—essential certitude—correlated to the human mind, and brought to cognition not through intuition but by reason.

Still, read this way, Plato's claims become *absolute* claims concerning the *necessity* of being in-itself. This kernel would be handed to Kant as he reconciled the schools of rationalism and empiricism. Or, as Kant would put it, "Can metaphysics come forward as an a priori science?" The problem to be resolved is whether there is an absolute whose nature is one of complete ontological authority and whether we can *know* that absolute as it is in-itself.

Meillassoux explains that, "Correlationism as I define it is not an anti-realism but an anti-absolutism."[8] Meillassoux in fact does embrace an absolutism, however it is one which firstly proceeds from the event (contingency), and secondly, it does not displace thought with respect to being. Thus, Meillassoux's ontology admits an absolute truth—but it is absolute truth of the necessity of contingency. He writes, "I will thus attempt to explain a nodal and seemingly paradoxical thesis [...] that there is only a history of the eternal, because only the eternal proceeds from the event. In other words: there is only a history of truths insofar as all truth is strictly eternal and impossible to reduce to any relativism."[9] In the name of rejecting absolutism tout court, many 20th-century Continental philosophers would fault the *dogmatic* nature of the absolute—especially in its spiritualized presentation. The danger perceived by 20th-century Continental philosophers (Heidegger, Derrida, Foucault, etc.) was that essentialist lines of thinking—meaning essential certitude in the form of a spiritualized absolute with ontological authority—necessarily results in *ontological dogmatism*.

2.3 Metaphysics after Kant

Kant had inherited two competing positions in empiricism and rationalism where rationalism regarded knowledge of reality *dogmatically* and empiricism *skeptically*. Kant's "Copernican revolution" was to synthesize these two positions in his critical philosophy. This synthesis was possible due to the question Kant set out to address in his *Critique of Pure Reason*: whether or not a priori knowledge of the world alone is possible (rationalism), or, whether any knowledge of an *intelligible* world must be grasped through sensibility (empiricism), in which case our knowledge would not be a priori. Kant's revolutionary answer found that we can have a priori knowledge about the structure of the sensible world but only because the sensible world is not entirely independent of the human mind. That is, the sensible world is *constructed* by the mind in terms of the mind synthesizing the empirical data it receives within the forms of its a priori categories. Knowledge of the world as independent of experience, a priori knowledge, was possible only insofar as the human mind itself contributed to it. Kant admits that the concepts of the mind would be empty without perceptions of experience, per the empiricists; yet the perceptions of experience would be blind if not for the concepts contributed by the mind, per the rationalists.

The "revolution" in question was, tellingly, *the priority of the thought-being correlate*, here understood as subject (thought) and object (being) where the subject (thought) is always already center. Lawrence Cahoone explains: "Just as Copernicus shifted the sun to the center of the universe, displacing the Earth from its Ptolemaic, geocentric home, Kant argued that rather than our knowledge conforming to objects, experienced objects *must* conform to our ways of knowing. The order of our reality is constructed, contributed by our own minds [...] This means that [...] knowledge of things in themselves independent of our senses, is permanently unavailable."[10] Thus, rather than the mind conforming to the external objects of sense experience, the objects of sense experience must conform to the intelligible structures of mind. This in itself was the beginning of Kant's transcendental idealism and would prove to be an essential link to transcendental phenomenology as practiced by Edmund Husserl.

The anti-absolutist, anti-essentialist thrust of Kant's philosophy was intended to temper dogmatic claims about things in themselves, that is, the world as it is in itself as completely independent of the conditions of sensibility. There could be no unmitigated or immediate access to a super-sensible realm (access through divine recollection, intuition, or pure reason) without some measure of experience informing it. Nor could one access a super-sensible realm beyond or behind phenomenal appearances. Because a priori categories of the human mind frame any empirical content, a world completely independent of the conditions of intelligibility is unknown. The activity of the mind and the given manifold of appearances must come together in a synthesis in order to construct the world as we know it. And the world as we know it cannot be known meaningfully any other way, for anything else would be to step outside of the conditions of our very knowing. On this account, then, any supposed necessary truth as to what the essential nature of the world is in itself is unavailable—a "I know not what." Against dogmatism there could be no One, True, Absolute essential X known in itself (the noumenal world). But against skepticism, there *could* be purchase upon the uniformity of appearances given the general structure of our knowing categories (how the phenomenal world must appear).

Kant's claims of finitude regarding the world or thing in itself (*das Ding an sich*) did not leave his system entirely impotent however, for with the Copernican revolution in place he moved from critical to practical philosophy (and later, this in turn would only exacerbate the problem of correlationism as Fichte picked up Kant's practical philosophy within his own subjective idealism). While we could not know the world in itself Kant reasoned that in terms of practical action it was still reasonable to act *as if* certain truths applied. That is, one could have faith in a certain kind of world and therefore act so as to achieve it because of the *rationality* of the belief in the possibility of achieving it. The practical truths of reason were thus not essentially nor absolutely true but instead functioned as "regulative ideas" employed by reason—ideas naturally supplied by reason so that human beings could make sense of their lived experience, in particular moral, political, and religious experience, and continue on living by the demands of "freedom, God, and immortality." Or as Kant famously put it, "I have denied knowledge in order to make room for faith." If we can conceive of an objective and absolute good in-itself and freely choose it *while recognizing our ability to choose or not choose*, then we can agree to universally assent to such a good in the attempt to bring it about if that absolute is at least logically possible, knowing that such an end or goal may never be achieved in this world. And the result is what Meillassoux titles "fideism"—"by forbidding reason any claim to the absolute the end of metaphysics has taken the form of an exacerbated return to the religious."[11]

Given that phenomenal appearances can only be structured according to so many logical-categorical forms (the table of judgments, the table of categories), the question naturally arises as to what occurs if different normative *content* is expressed through those categories and their forms of judgment? What if the veracity of the appearances themselves differs regarding which ideals are worth believing in?

2.4 From Finitude to Perspectivalism and Anti-Realism

It is not the *structure* of the Kantian categories which is problematic. The problem for Kant is the *plurality* of the *meaning of appearances*. It was Nietzsche who argued that Kantian appearances were always *interpreted*, usually toward some practical end. And the ultimate practical end for any living being is its own survival. In the quest to affirm one's own ends, one's own survival, Nietzsche claimed that one's own perspective must be affirmed through the imaginative (cunning) effort to survive. Thus inevitable distortions and obfuscations take place as acts of interpretation narrow one's vision to their own perspective. And so a certain will-to-life or vitalistic urge replaced Kantian rationality as the measure of practical ends and self-affirmation. Reason was no longer self-grounding or self-legislating—what mattered was the ability to arbitrate one appearance over another, to strategically determine by way of *power* and self-mastery what "noble lie" (rather than "regulative Ideal") one would choose to believe. Nietzsche claimed (drawing upon the earlier claims of Schopenhauer) that the will itself was fundamentally *irrational*. Life itself has no ultimate *telos*, goal, or purpose other than the self-affirmation of what is living—exclusively at the expense of *other* living things.

In many ways, Nietzsche's own rejection of Platonic metaphysics, an opening he found through the relativizing of perspective brought on by the Kantian embrace of finitude, was the true predecessor to 20th-century anti-absolutist philosophy. Nietzsche after all thought to philosophize with a hammer. He wished to smash the idols of classical Platonic philosophy: its belief in an intelligible or supernatural world beyond this one; its belief in objective knowledge independent of the knower; its belief in the unity of the human self or soul; its belief in the univocity of sense and meaning; and its belief in the very notion of truth as eternal and necessary.

Nietzsche's philosophy in this way is, as Heidegger pointed out, Platonism turned on its head. But Kantian finitude meant *fideism*, "faith" where knowledge ended at the limit of phenomenal appearance. And here Nietzsche too succumbs to the fideist position: "faith" only meant resolve toward life lived willfully, artfully, and practically without the false pretenses assumed by the desires of reason. Nietzsche demonstrated that the correlation of human and world, or perspective and reality, was absolutely *necessary* and hence *inevitable*. One could not outstrip one's own interested perspective through any use of reason: meaning, all is relative and all is perspective. "We are human, all too human."

Nietzsche's influence upon 20th-century Continental philosophy cannot be underestimated as he is arguably postmodernism's chief progenitor in not only ratcheting Kantian epistemological finitude into an ontological perspectivalism but also in his utter rejection of and contempt for any Parmenidean or Platonic absolute. Indeed, without Nietzsche the phenomenon known as "postmodernism" cannot be said to have occurred.

Prior to the height of postmodern Continental philosophy, occurring during the late 20th century, Nietzsche's challenge to absolutism found an unlikely ally in the existential philosophy of Søren Kierkegaard. And it was Kierkegaard who was translated into German and read by a philosopher who is widely regarded to be among the most important, if not *the* most important, Continental philosopher of the 20th century: Martin Heidegger. The "philosophy of existence"—found in Nietzsche, Kierkegaard, and Heidegger, but also in Sartre or Camus, looks upon a world without any transcendental meaning, meaning, purpose of direction. Rejecting the Platonic notion of an absolute truth with a fixed eternal essence, existentialism emphasized *existence* over essence. Without the spiritual certitude afforded by Platonic metaphysics existentialists sought to base any degree of so-called "certainty" in the actual choices of human beings rather than in other-worldly ultimates. Authenticity, angst, and despair were corollaries of the loss of essentialist notions of truth and as the old Platonic metaphysics crumbled away existentialists and others thought that there could be nothing more positively liberating than this philosophy of freedom and human action.

Nietzsche's belief was that in our attempt to explain reality we in fact *constitute* it. He believed that those disciplines whose pretense is to find an objective and neutral standpoint are themselves "decentered" in their very attempt to ground a rational or objective standpoint, for a constituted (and presupposed) objective center already haunts the claim of their position. That is, before a concrete position of objectivity can be claimed a *difference* of *constituting appearances* endlessly reconstitutes the world in an arbitrary process. Without an essential or eternal absolute of some kind beforehand there is no objective world: just the differentiating process of various appearances in competition with one another. Nietzsche's discovery that language, logic, and science were *relative* to the perspective meant that a perceiver was already buried in surrounding conditions of appearance. There could be no transcendental support for whatever truth or fact the perceiver was attempting to obtain.

According to the tradition that followed, the essentialist metaphysics challenged by Nietzsche was a metaphysics of "presence": a metaphysics purporting to know absolutely the ultimate foundations of reality independent of human categories and values, human history, human language, human culture and meaning. Heidegger for example in the opening chapter of *Being and Time* (1927) was fearful that the human pretension to know Being as a specific kind of beings was in fact a hubris of thought gone unchecked. It was because of the tendency to see reality as nothing more than a collection of substances standing ready for data collection and analysis that deeper questions concerning existence itself were left covered up. This in fact fueled Heideggerean paranoia toward the technological sciences in its perceived effort to "totalize" Being—Being now conceived within a *Gestell*: a utilitarian framework of "standing reserve" where first beings were thought within the category of substantial objects *to be used*, thus whose nature is not fundamentally *self-according* but *self-affording* (to the uses of human beings). In one sense one might claim Heidegger did advocate a kind of realism in his own challenge to essentialist metaphysics for he loathed how the manner of the sciences could be interpreted as concealing the disclosure of Being in or on its own terms rather than strictly within the terms as set forth by the human sciences. On the other hand, Heidegger advocated that *only* through *Dasein* could any disclosure or unconcealment of Being take place. Heidegger nevertheless followed Nietzsche in rejecting science as the Archimedean viewpoint upon reality as he considered "reason" to be "the most stiff-necked adversary of thinking."

Already we can see how the relative value of an interpreted nature of appearances could lead to the disciplines of hermeneutics and deconstruction (although of course Nietzsche influences the *entire* tradition of 20th-century Continental philosophy). Especially appealing was the Nietzschean idea that a text, or nature read as text, always deals with a *pre-given* meaning of a text. Heidegger's identification of the hermeneutical circle acknowledged the always already historical and hence prejudicial nature of these meanings through human "facticity"—that *Dasein* was always already "thrown into a world," is always already *part* of the world historically that one chooses to understand (for Merleau-Ponty, for example, who took Heidegger a step further, we are always already part of an "environment" which co-constitutes us as we co-constitute it, we are always already embodied). Further, Derrida, drawing upon both Nietzsche and Heidegger, attempted to allow the self-destabilizing nature of claims to truth unfold in his method of *deconstruction*. Here Derrida took cue from Heidegger's call to "dismantle" the history of *Dasein* prejudiced pre-understanding of the nature and meaning of the history of Being. However, for Derrida, after any dismantling or deconstructing no one essential, present identity for truth or reality could be found. Only difference remains.

Overall, Nietzsche's major contribution to all of existential, hermeneutic, and deconstructive philosophy was then this: we cannot begin from an entirely presuppositionless standpoint and existence cannot be understood in any "neutral" terms. *One always approaches their existence from a specific perspective or viewpoint influenced by factors of which the individual may not even be aware.* Through a tradition stemming from Kant, then, we can see how Nietzsche and Heidegger both embraced finitude so as to combat absolutizing and totalizing claims upon the nature of reality or Being. Kant's limitation of human knowledge to phenomenal appearances secured an open space of possibility for the creation of meaning over and against any pre-determined authoritative (or eternal, necessary, spiritual) truth. Yet, the cost of this was realism itself.

To conclude our historical presentation of correlationist subject-at-center metaphysics and its subsequent development and impact on 20th-century Continental philosophy, the stated goal of this chapter has been to show how it was Kant's reconciliation of rationalism and empiricism that planted the notion of ontological necessity within the kernel of subject-at-center ontology. This development began with Parmenides, worked its way through Plato, was picked up by Descartes, was anchored in appearance and will by Nietzsche, but most importantly had an absolute degree of necessity planted within it by Kant. Nietzsche then linked this necessity with the relativity of appearances and their interpretation. Beginning with Kantian metaphysics, then, is the era that Meillassoux would call "The Era of Correlationism." Nietzsche helped to solidify the era of correlationism as one that is also anti-realist in its orientation being perspectivalist and relativist. These positions radicalized Kant's position concerning the finitude of the human perspective and its purchase upon reality.

Ontological finitude came with the cost of affirming an always-already given (a priori) correlate between thought and being or between subject and object, and affirming thought as opposed to being without thought (the noumenal realm); in other words, we have briefly traced the birth of Kantian transcendental idealism as fodder for 20th-century Continental anti-realism. The conclusion is that, with Kant as its predecessor postmodern Continental philosophy (whose roots go back to Nietzsche and Heidegger), anti-realist correlationism denied any knowledge of the real in-itself claiming that reality is always already co-related to the conditions of human experience; and indeed, that any real in-itself is always already co-related to human beings in some *context-dependent way*; how it is accessed under the inextricable human-centered conditions which taint it whether through the categories of the understanding, the will to power, invariant existential categories, sign or text, language and discursive formation, or categories of social construction.

For 20th-century Continental philosophy existence or reality in-itself is always *as-it-is-for-us*. Or still further, the in-itself is not simply an unknown Kantian noumenal postulate, the most extreme of postmodernism would suggest that there is no one reality behind appearances to postulate. All becomes collapsed phenomenologically into the givenness of experience, of one's own perspective. In following Kant, then, the most decisive decision in Continental philosophy was to remain within a domain of *human finitude*. In as simple of terms possible it was Kant who first securely limited reality to the "transparent cage of consciousness and language," to the *a priori categories of the human mind*.

Resources for Further Reading

Backman, Jussi, "Transcendental Idealism and Strong Correlationism: Meillassoux and the End of Heideggerian Finitude," in *Phenomenology and the Transcendental*, edited by Sara Heinämaa, Mirja Hartimo, and Timo Miettinen (New York & London: Routledge): 276–295.

Brassier, Raymond, "That Which Is Not: Plato, Kant, and Sellars," SCT Public Event at Cornell University, July 10, 2012 (also presented in May 2012 as part of the "Contemporary Materialism, Realism, and Metaphysics" Berlin Workshop), available online: http://afterxnature.blogspot.com/p/after-nature-podcasts-mp3-downloads.html.

Braver, Lee, *A Thing of this World: History of Continental Anti-Realism* (Evanston, IL: Northwestern University Press, 2007).

Carli, Riccardo, "Relational Ontology in Nietzsche: An Introduction," *Parrhesia* 26 (2016): 96–116: http://www.parrhesiajournal.org/parrhesia26/parrhesia26_carli.pdf .

Ferraris, Maurizio, *Goodbye, Kant!: What Still Stands of the Critique of Pure Reason*, translated by Richard Davies (New York: SUNY Press, 2013).

Gironi, Fabio, "What Has Kant Ever Done for Us? Speculative Realism and the Kantian Heritage," in *Breaking the Spell: Contemporary Realism under Discussion*, edited by Anna Longo and Sarah De Sanctis (Mimesis, 2015). Available online: https://www.academia.edu/6510568/What_Has_Kant_Ever_Done_for_Us_Speculative_Realism_and_the_Kantian_Heritage.

Notes

1. Badiou in *After Finitude*, vii.
2. Meillassoux, *After Finitude*, 5.
3. Meillassoux, *Time without Becoming*.
4. Levi Bryant, Nick Srnicek, Graham Harman, eds., *The Speculative Turn: Continental Realism and Materialism* (Melbourne: re.press, 2011), 4.
5. Bryant, Srnicek, and Harman, *The Speculative Turn*, 4.
6. Meillassoux, *After Finitude*, 44.
7. Grant, *Philosophies of Nature after Schelling*, viii.
8. Meillassoux, "Time without Becoming."
9. Quentin Meillassoux, "History and Event," in Alain Badiou.
10. Lawrence E. Cahoone, ed., *From Modernism to Postmodernism: An Anthology*, 2nd ed. (Malden: Blackwell, 2003), 45.
11. Meillassoux, *After Finitude*, 45.

III
After Finitude

3.1 Correlationism and the Goal of *After Finitude*

MEILLASSOUX'S *AFTER FINITUDE* (2007, TRANSLATED BY Ray Brassier in 2008) has as its central claim the call to return to a metaphysics of the absolute. As discussed in the previous chapter, it was Continental philosophy's aversion of the absolute and penchant for anti-absolutist thinking which brought about the renunciation of claims upon reality in itself. This anti-absolutism in turn led to various forms of anti-realism and anti-essentialism— in short the rejection of any claims upon truth and the rejection of the very possibility of metaphysics. And, as we have determined, for Meillassoux, claim upon the absolute does not necessarily involve pretenses of ontological dogmatism, especially of the sort rebuffed by the major figures of the 20th century—Heidegger, Derrida, Foucault, etc. For Meillassoux, a philosophy of the absolute rejects ontological dogmatism taken upon faith (fideism, creationism) as well as dogmatic metaphysics which *assert* rather than attempt to *demonstrate* the possibility of speculative claims. Meillassoux does claim that a kind of absolute philosophy (what he calls "absolutist materialism" or "speculative materialism") is possible by way of metaphysics-as-speculation. This in turn can make possible the kind of non-naive realism he claims we are able to attain and thus "get outside of ourselves to grasp the in-itself."[1] This is in other words to say that Meillassoux does follow the speculative gesture initiated by Hegel to proceed into the Open "after" or perhaps "beyond" Kantian finitude and its absorption of the real into the concrete limits of human experience. But while Meillassoux follows the Hegelian speculative gesture he denies any Hegelian necessitation of the correlate between thought and being itself, as we shall see in this chapter.

The goal of Meillassoux's *After Finitude* is as simple as it is revolutionary: *re-activate a philosophy of the absolute by re-asserting the absolutizing capacity of thought*. This shall be made possible by thinking a being which is absolutely independent of thought, that is, a being unaffected by our mode of apprehending that being in subjectivity. This occurs when we consider the contingency of our own being in the correlation between being and thought (whether post or prior to the correlation), and discover that contingency itself is the only absolutely necessary form of being. That is, what turns out to be absolute is not the correlation between thought and being but the very *fact* of the correlation's necessarily contingent existence.

To review why Meillassoux would make this argument, in the last chapter we determined that in the post-Kantian tradition, absorbed within the finite range of human experience (cognitive, normative, or otherwise) was the real in-itself—that is, the real as it is independent, apart, and non-correlated to human beings and all that human beings bring to the table. Whether referred to as the Absolute, the Unconditioned, the Real, or the "Absolute Outside," reality was claimed to be always given-as-appearance in some way. The repercussions of this claim resulted in an anthropocentric epistemological framework limiting query to the various normative—existential or phenomenological—and interpretive—hermeneutic or deconstructive—dimensions of human experience. Inquiry was always inquiry through a "cage of subjectivity," so to speak. In Kantian terms, an outside could not be known apart from the universal forms of subjectivity which render reality *experience-as-such*, that is to say, reality's "givenness" was always given-as a specific subject-at-center appearance. And, as we have established, the ontological finitude secured by Kant's Copernican revolution instituted an "Era of Correlation": as Meillassoux has quite boldly claimed: "We cannot but be heirs of Kantianism."[2] The conclusion to be drawn here is that Kantian finitude debars any attainment of the absolute, a reality "whose separateness from thought is such that it presents itself to us as non-relative [...] absolute truth solely through its own resources."[3] How does Meillassoux make his argument concerning the absolute? In this case we must first draw several distinctions as made in Meillassoux's philosophy but also as used in their normal capacity in order to see how Meillassoux's position is *realist* as much as it is *speculative*.

It must be stated that the anti-absolutist and anti-essentialist philosophies of Continental philosophy in the 20th century were not specifically *irrealist* or *solipsists* in their anti-realism. While Continental philosophy largely claimed that the world is always co-related to the subject perceiving or interpreting the world, this does not mean that the philosophers under discussion here claimed that the world or the objects in it *depend upon* consciousness for their existence. How exactly the conscious subject relates to the objects of phenomenal appearance was the matter taken up by the other most important philosophy of the 20th century, namely the school of phenomenology founded by Edmund Husserl. Meillassoux does not for the most part explicitly identify phenomenology as the correlationist's philosophy par excellence, but the subtext is there. Further, it is phenomenology's connection to Kantian transcendental idealism which problematizes the very task phenomenology sets out to accomplish: returning to the "things themselves," albeit always as perceived within the givenness of conscious experience and hence phenomenal appearance.

The question to be answered here is whether phenomenology is indeed simply an anti-realism and correlationist philosophy (to push further, a form of *subjective idealism*) or if in fact phenomenology may ever be properly speculative (or in the past, for example with Hegel, was phenomenology ever properly speculative). As Meillassoux has claimed that "our task consists in trying to understand how thought is able to access the uncorrelated

[...] a world capable of subsisting without being given," we ought not to assume that Meillassoux believes that a speculative phenomenology is impossible *if* there is a way in which phenomenology can access the uncorrelated or if by the very definition of phenomenology's self-proclaimed task it is doomed to correlationist failure. In other words, we must ask whether—by methodologically linking thought necessarily to the world as a world always "given-as-conscious appearance"—phenomenology results in some form of idealism, whether transcendental or subjective idealism where there is a necessary methodological connection between the world and the conscious experience of that world in the subjective form of appearance.

Perfectly compatible with (speculative) materialism, Meillassoux believes that "thought can think being that is independent of thought" and that indeed it *may* be possible for phenomenology to accomplish this if it is properly naturalized or mathematized (it is interesting to note here that C.S. Peirce sees phenomenology as a branch of mathematics, a speculative-metaphysical science and that recently Alain Badiou, Meillassoux's former teacher, has turned to Peirce to mine such an approach). Meillassoux writes for example that, "Phenomenology remains for me a formidable descriptive enterprise of the complexities of the given [...] we ought to protect the richness with which it restores to our experience of the sensible."[4] By this Meillassoux seems to be inferring that rather than follow the "tricks and denials" of phenomenologists who operate in the idealist-vein (for him Husserl, Heidegger, and Sartre) we must distinguish between a phenomenology of the Berkeleyan or solipsist type and the type that affirms the sensible materiality of "ancestral realities" independent of thought yet which are accessible to it.[5] For as much as Meillassoux derides subjective pole of the correlation it is nevertheless the question of *the emergence* of subjectivity (its "creation" or "advent") which preoccupies his discussion of the advent of worlds which culminates in justice through a quasi-Hegelian progression of worlds: matter to life to thought, and then to the Fourth World of Justice. In other words, Meillassoux's implicit critique of the subjectivation of materiality outside ought not lead us to believe that there is absolutely no room for subjectivity in the ethical or theological dimension of his metaphysics. He is, rather, critiquing a specific *kind* of phenomenology as much as he critiques a specific *kind* of absolutism (dogmatic or fideistic-creationist) and anti-absolutism (relativism, anti-realism). As James Bradley has noted in speaking of what relates Meillassoux's speculative endeavor to those such as Whitehead's or Peirce's, when it comes to the topic of phenomenology one may distinguish between speculative *description* and speculative *explanation*. We shall return to the theme of phenomenology later in this chapter, however for now let us turn to examine the meaning of correlationism itself more closely as we draw several important distinctions that Meillassoux makes qualifying his philosophy as a "speculative" or "absolute" materialism.

The philosophy of Quentin Meillassoux is predominantly a philosophy in which he seeks to confront Kantian finitude and proceed "after" or beyond it. Meillassoux's neologism for Kantian finitude is "correlationism." Correlationism is the view that "there are no objects, no events, no laws, no beings which are not always-already correlated with a point of view, with a subjective access." Subject and object, thought and being, only come as a pair related where access to either term of the correlate alone is deemed either contradictory or impossible. Thus the subject-object, mind-world, thought-being relation is fundamentally *representational* in that the world is "always-already" *given* or primarily represented, manifested, to the subject. One may think of subject and object or being and thought as *necessarily coupled* in this regard. In fact, in *After Finitude* Meillassoux defines correlation in that very way: "Correlationism consists in disqualifying the claim that it is possible to consider the realms of subjectivity and objectivity independently of one another."[6]

Meillassoux is clear to point out that *Dasein* and world, language and referent, consciousness and phenomenal appearance, phenomena and noumena, interpreter and interpretant, noetic and noematic, mind and world all are couplings in correlationist ontologies. For the correlationist there is "nothing outside of the text"—no way to escape the circle of the correlation and know that which is anything outside of an always-already co-given relation. This is not to say that for some correlationists (such as Kant) things do not *exist* outside of what is co-related to the subjective access of consciousness, we cannot just *know* what they are in and of themselves or apart from the manner in which they are given under the conditions of consciousness. In each case the correlation is posted as prior fact which renders thought deabsolutized.

As an "always-already" or primordial co-givenness we may say that there is a transcendental core of correlationism. This core serves as metaphysical a priori, finds its way into Husserl and in more exaggerated form in Sartre, where the very identity of subject and object or consciousness and world derive their identity from the other. One cannot be said to be a "subject" if not for the contents of consciousness: the world. Yet there cannot be a "world" save for consciousness intending it (in phenomenology nothing is non-intentional: consciousness is always conscious "of" something, hence the definition of "intentionality"). Again, this is not to detract from the realist moments in phenomenology which do not claim that the world's existence somehow depends upon perception *to be*. On the other hand, the ontological difference between Being and beings is *constitutive* of any being's identity—and this establishes the always-already given identity of relation between any two beings. Here the "co" of "co-relation" is the primordial element over any strictly given terms. As in each case, whether phenomenological appearance or ontological difference, the emphasis is on essential relatedness—even if established by a real ontological difference "between" entities.

Meillassoux's term for his own philosophy is that of "speculative" or "absolute materialism." "Speculation" for Meillassoux means any philosophy which claims to attain the absolute outside of thought. Being also a philosopher of *realism* he states that due to the primacy of correlated reality *to* human consciousness "We have lost the great outdoors."[7] In place of correlationism, then, he advocates for a speculative or "absolute materialism," the view that "every thought acceding to an absolute that is external to thought and which is itself devoid of all subjectivity." Meillassoux's argument is straightforward: absolute reality has no subjective, psychological, egoic, vital traits whatsoever. Absolute reality is that of an absolutist materialism for *there is no subjective character to it in itself*. By contrast, any *non-materialist* form of absolutism makes the correlation itself absolute, for example, in Hegel. Unlike Hegel however, Meillassoux argues that in his philosophy he does not dogmatically proclaim "what is," but only speaks of "what can be." Whatever matter is, it is not subjective—but he has no theory of matter as such. Thus, following his reasoning one should conclude that absolutist materialism is a non-dogmatic absolute.

3.2 Strong and Weak Correlationism

There are two main arguments concerning the correlation: the first is the "correlationist circle" and the second is "correlational facticity."

The correlationist circle is where a vicious pragmatic circle circumscribes reality stating that as soon as one thinks of something "outside" of thought that "outside" is instantly itself converted into a thought. So in a "two step" procedure the immediacy of any object other than thought is immediately taken over by thought being always-already co-related to it. As Meillassoux explains,

"Generally speaking, the modern philosopher's 'two-step' consists in this belief in the primacy of the relation over the related terms [...] The 'co' (of co-givenness, of co-relation, of the co-originary, of co-presence, etc.) is the grammatical particle that dominates modern philosophy, its veritable 'chemical formula.'"[8] Therefore the correlationist circle involves the *transcendental co-givenness* between thought and being and this establishes the veritable impossibility of exiting *through* thought—through the correlation—to any being which could be said to be *independent of thought*. So we never have access to any independent thing not always already correlated to an act of thinking it. As soon as we try to think of something independent of our thinking that thing is drawn back into the circle.

The position that one cannot think of any thing which is not thought, or that it is a contradiction in terms to say that somehow one can "think the unthought," necessarily entails an anti-materialist (idealist) position. On the pain of contradiction the correlationist claims that to think the unthought or to think something "independent of" thought is still *thought*. For the correlationist "We cannot think a world without an entity that is capable of thinking it."[9]

The second argument of correlation is "correlational facticity." This maintains that the closure of thought upon itself is not a symptom of thought's finitude but is a result of the correlation's ontological necessity. If thought cannot exit apart from a non-subjective material reality then this is because it discovers itself as an intrinsically necessary reality.[10] Here speculation claims to have survived the finitude posed by the correlational circle by remaining within the Absolute itself, and the result is Absolute Idealism. Whereas in the correlationist circle there could be admitted in the first step an "in itself" (to be immediately drawn into the circle), here the circle *itself* becomes the absolute. The absolute is the very condition of the subject-object correlate. Now, Meillassoux actually uses correlational facticity in his own argument concerning the absolute and even grants its necessity, however he does so not to say that speculatively this means the correlation itself is necessary but only that the absolute is found in the very conditions of the correlate which is, itself, *necessarily contingent*.

Meillassoux argues that the correlationist is the opponent of any true realism where even the naive realist operates within the correlationist circle of thought; and thus, too, is a correlationist. Here the naive realist, in stating that it is possible to attain reality in itself "as existing independently of his viewpoint" still defines reality's independence in terms of a subject-object correlation, that is, in terms of a subjective viewpoint. The external world is still "given" in its independence *from the subject*. The "circle" of correlation is quite simply the argument that in speaking of reality whether inside the mind (or for the naive realist, outside of the mind) reality is nevertheless *posited* in being spoken about. "When you speak against the correlation, you forget that you speak against the correlation."[11] So even in refuting the dependence of the world upon the subject the correlation still encloses the subject *as its negated term*. For this reason

Meillassoux states that the correlation simply cannot be abandoned but instead must be *worked through*.

Opposite to naive realism would be the postmodern rejection of realism in anti-realism. In this sort of correlationism all is happily embraced by the circle of correlation and to say anything otherwise is to turn what is supposedly "outside of thought" into a thought, for one cannot perceive beyond the limits of one's own subjectivity. As was discussed in the last chapter, Nietzsche served as a prime example that there is no reality conceivable apart from the perspective, mind, language, culture, or practice accessing it, for that reality is always thought by and through *a perspective*, thought by a mind, spoken via a language, evaluated in terms of a culture, or approached by a subject, an "all too human" subject. And thus the importance of Nietzsche's approach to and subsequent development of the Kantian subject-at-center metaphysics certainly cannot be underestimated. Expressed in a different context, the bite of this argument, employed by Fichte against Kant, claims that it is senseless to speak of an "in-itself" apart from the phenomenal reach of consciousness, for the "in-itself" was still *known* even in its noumenal character as a positive phenomenal appearance of consciousness, namely the thing-in-itself (*das Ding an sich*). This is why Fichte believed that all could be contained by an Absolute conceived of as Ego (*Ich*), the ultimate or most encompassing fact of subjectivity.

Meillassoux advocates for a speculative position of *realism* that breaks with the correlationist's circle. Traditionally defined, for the realist there is a world external to and independent of thought. This is fundamentally an epistemological thesis in that there is an objective world external to the subject that can be known independently as an external reality. As an epistemological thesis idealism would deny the externality of this supposed relation stating that the world in some degree is circumscribed by thought: whether completely and individually as in the case of solipsism, or to the human mind as such, as in the case of subjective idealism. Objective idealism on the other hand would not necessarily deny that there is an "external" world but may state that in it ideas are in fact very much real and perhaps take on primary reality-status.

It should be noted that as metaphysical theses, realism is often paired with materialism as the external world is in itself fundamentally of a physical, material nature; whereas for idealism the "really" real world is fundamentally spiritual or mind-like. In terms of knowledge governing these pictures of reality the realist may or may not be a nominalist: the view that universals in their ideal nature are "real" (as Plato could very well be considered a metaphysical realist concerning the nature of universals but is also in some sense an idealist, given his epistemology).

Idealists typically are not nominalist as their "really" real world is of the idea and has no issue accommodating the reality of the universal, whether within nature (as an objective idealist would) or within a transcendental plane of subjectivity or spirit (as Plato would). Here the mediating position between objective and subjective idealism would be Kant's transcendental idealism which claims that there are a priori structures of the human mind which renders in what ways the external world may be known, but knowledge of the external world *in-itself* is impossible given these same a priori mental-categorical structures.

Each of these positions is inherently dualistic in several respects, and Meillassoux breaks down each of them exposing the dependence of the subject-object relation. Even the realist must maintain that there is a knowing subject whose nature, however dependent upon an external material world it is, nevertheless possesses a subjectivity which must be explained in terms of that material world. On the other hand, the idealist, even in subjective idealism (that is not a solipsism), must argue that the external world of matter is only apparent and can be converted back into the substance of the idea. Thus, the realism/idealism scheme necessarily involves a subject and object relationship. Subjectivity and objectivity define each other (subjects perceive objects; objects are objects because they are perceived). In that relationship subjectivity and objectivity cannot be analyzed apart from their co-defining particle (the "co" in "correlation), as what would subjectivity be if not subjectivity for some kind of objectivity. And vice versa.

From here Meillassoux is able to take the next step of his argument: divide correlationism into two main types or versions—a "strong" version and a "weak" version.

First, Kantian transcendental idealism can be identified as a "weak" correlationism. The reason is that philosophy is not prohibited from the absolute although the absolute is unknowable. "According to Kant, we know *a priori* that the thing-in-itself is non-contradictory and that it actually exists."¹² We do not know however the absolute's true nature for only within the a priori circle of thought can the world be given and rendered. There cannot be a world truly understood apart from the a priori manner in which we know it. And so there is a noumenal realm which is responsible for the phenomenal appearances of consciousness and which themselves serve to be representations of such a world. But the key here is *that there is* a noumenal world, a world in-itself. We cannot know what that world in itself is however due to the very conditions of our knowing. In other words, the correlation between subject and object which is always already present in the categories of human understanding serves as the bars of the cage which we might see through were it not for the mental categories rendering reality as such. Stated differently, there can be no nature which is not already correlated to an act of thought.

"Strong" correlationism circumscribes the Kantian noumenal within the circle of thought and states, along with Fichte, that we cannot even know the thing in-itself as something "in-itself" or utterly and absolutely other than subject or Ego. Whereas weak correlationism has followed Kant in insisting on the finitude of reason and our conditional access to reality, strong correlationism, as pointed out by Hegel, claims that Kant has "already overstepped the boundary between knowable and unknowable in presuming that the structure of things-in-themselves differs from the structure of phenomena."¹³ As Brassier explains, "Hegel will proceed to re-inject that which is transcendentally 'for us' *back into the in-itself* [...] [T]hinking grounds its own access to being and rediscovers its intrinsic infinitude."[14] Thus, "Where Kant's weak correlationism emphasizes the uncircumventable contingency inherent in the correlation between thinking and being, Hegelianism absolutizes the correlation and thereby insists on the necessary isomophy between the structure of thinking and that of being."[15]

Meillassoux (and in concert Brassier), identify a "speculative idealism" where the "in itself" disappears. The thought-world correlation is itself absolutized in the necessity of the correlation: being itself *becomes thought*. Such is a way to decouple the subject and object Meillassoux admits, yet all becomes subject in being enveloped by it. As Meillassoux puts it, in strong correlationism there is "an essential inseparability of the act of thinking from its content. All we engage with is what is given-to-thought, never an entity subsisting itself."[16] Here though *there is no entity that subsists in-itself which is <u>not</u> thought*. The "in-itself" is "abolished."[17]

Now, on the one hand the absolute idealism of Hegel (and not his speculative method) may be seen as a prime representative of strong correlationism, but more tellingly, Meillassoux points out that when any form of subjectivity hypostatizes the subjective side of the correlate term, then strong correlationism is the result. "Accordingly, it will be maintained that the notion of the in-itself is devoid of truth because it is unthinkable, and that it should be abolished so that only the relation between subject and object remains [...] A metaphysics of this type may select from among various forms of subjectivity, but it is invariably characterized by the fact that it hypostatizes some mental, sentient, or vital term: representation in the Leibnizian monad; Schelling's Nature, or the objective subject-object; Hegelian Mind; Schopenhauer's Will; the Will to Power in Nietzsche; perception loaded with memory in Bergson; Deleuze's Life, etc."[18] In all of these a determinate human access to the world is already subjectively pre-given, for all relations are always already a relation to subject (perceiver, observer, experiencing being) where subject then becomes Being itself, the absolute. Perception, willing, experiencing is turned into the absolute. "Since we cannot conceive a being which would not be constituted by our relation to the world since we cannot escape from the circle of correlation—the whole of these relations, or an eminent part of this whole, represents the very essence of reality."[19] Every objective representation is re-inscribed within the correlationist circle. In the strongest sense of this kind of correlationism then, one cannot think the unthought for to think what is unthought is itself a thought.

At this stage Meillassoux states that he will now refer to strong correlationism as a "subjectalism." Any refutation of absolute materialism is strong correlationism, yet within the lines of Kantian correlational facticity one may speculatively admit the possibility of materialism but at the expense of knowledge and capacity for thought (which is weak correlationism). Subjectalism consists in, as Meillassoux describes, "emphasizing subjectivity or some of its characteristics—will, perception, consciousness—so as to maintain a postmodern anti-materialism without renouncing the speculative status of philosophy." Thus, Meillassoux states that one can use the correlation in two different ways. First, one may claim that we are completely in the correlation and the correlation is an obstacle to the absolute. This is correlationism "proper" as on this view no one is able to know the absolute, the in-itself, being trapped within the correlation. Second, the correlation *itself* becomes the absolute and we cannot escape from it being already inside and part of the absolute. In either case the correlation is hypostatized.

What entices Meillassoux to "break" with the circle of correlation? Is the correlationist's move to reinstall transcendental subjectivity *back into* the absolute based upon a false premise of realism rather than correlated idealism? The subjectalist puts will, subjectivity, mind everywhere while speculatively maintaining a non-human nature. In this subjectalism has two poles: *vitalism*, which makes *life* encompassing category (for example Bergson, Nietzsche, Deleuze); and *idealism*, which makes *mind* or consciousness encompassing category (for example Schelling or Hegel, and under some interpretations idealist or transcendental phenomenology). Meillassoux does not oppose subjectalization as a speculative philosophy of the absolute insofar that it is a metaphysics of the Open.[20] But, he does oppose the subjectalization of the real as it is the absolutization of only a *part* of the correlation, that of subjectivity. On the account of Meillassoux's absolute or speculative materialism, reality is absolutely asubjective—this despite the fact that life and consciousness arise from it in eschatological advents; a nod back to Hegel who Meillassoux has said is his "secret master."[21] Let us now turn to the final step in Meillassoux's argument in order to assess his response to the correlationist.

3.3 Breaking with the Circle of Correlation: Facticity and Arche-Fossil

As we know, correlationism means that subject and object are always already co-related, coupled together as a pair. Each item, whether subject or object, therefore cannot be isolated so as to be known "in-itself" absolutely. Either term of the correlate cannot be isolated beyond the primordial fact of the always-already "primordial" nature of the correlate itself. In the stronger version of correlationism, "subjectalism," "substance becomes subject." The correlation itself is absolutized and one pole is hypostatized. In either case the material absolute, that is, matter without subjectivity, is thought to be an impossibility beyond the representation and givenness of correlated terms.

Meillassoux concludes that one can escape the correlation if we absolutize the *necessary contingency* of subjects and objects alike (the correlation) rather than hypostatize either pole necessarily (as in the case of subjectalism and strong correlationism: where the absolute is subjectivity; or in the case of weak correlationism: where the absolute is unknown because of the conditions of subjectivity). This is to say that, whatever constituting correlation is present, thought itself is able to attain an absolute outside by attaining the facticity of a *necessarily contingent* basis of correlation. How is this possible?

Meillassoux seeks to demonstrate the possibility of attaining the absolute outside independent of every subject by way of a speculative argument. By considering the form of "pure and simple death"—ontologically the "principle of facticity" or the fact that things can be otherwise than what they are—Meillassoux believes that one may demonstrate a necessarily contingent fact. By virtue of the fact that one can imagine one's life or ownmost being destroyed; that is, one can think of a complete decoupling from the correlation by first considering one's own death, Meillassoux believes that one has allowed an ontological contingency to be represented by the thought of death itself; this in order to demonstrate that one can attain *through thought a reality of an absence of thought.* And this may occur when considering the necessary eventuality of one's own death—the necessity of one's own contingent existence. The *fact* of one's death here allows for the employment of Meillasssoux's "principle of facticity"—just as our own non-being is possible (one's life is contingent and yet this contingency is necessary) the absolute in philosophy, which is not the correlation but a being we can now "think of as unthought," is given in the form of a being whose contingency is absolutely necessary. And so Meillassoux's *After Finitude* book has the title "The Necessity of Contingency" as the only necessary fact is contingency itself.

The principle of facticity consists in no longer absolutizing the correlation as in subjectalism or the circle of correlation as in correlationism, but in absolutizing correlational facticity itself. Facticity is "that which actualizes our non-being and contingency independent of our thought." Here Meillassoux argues that the correlationist must say there is a possibility for the correlation to disappear if in any meaningful sense the correlationist is to admit that there is a world that is not *merely* the internal representation of a subject. If the correlationist does not admit this their position sinks into subjectalism (either in the form of vitalism, idealism, or perhaps even spiritualism), postmodernism via strong correlationism, or solipsism (via radical subjective idealism: the world is merely "in" the mind). Meillassoux believes that he has found a way to the absolute because if one can think of the absolute destruction of subjectivity then one can think something which is utterly *independent* of it: the very *fact* of subjectivity's destruction and its non-being.

Meillassoux explains: "If you can think of the possibility of death that must be independent of your life to be thought, because if your death is merely a correlate of your subjectivity (a mere idea, presentation, appearance) which exists only as a correlate of what you think your death would depend upon your mere thinking a life. But, your death survives you because it destroys you. You can think the possibility of your own annihilation and this capacity is to think of yourself as contingent and this contingency is the only absolute necessity that there is."

Meillassoux believes that by seeing as *fact* that the correlation does not necessarily have to exist (it is necessarily contingent)—and this is possible to attain in the thought of one's own death or annihilation—then one is able to have a concept that is of the *real* "outside"—a kind of being which is absolutely independent of thought because *thought does not exist*. Attaining the non-being of thought given such an annihilation of thought is possible in two ways. First, we are able to scientifically and empirically assess a world *before human consciousness*, before life on this planet, or before the creation of the earth itself and any form of subjectivity associated with it. Reality would here be absent of any subjectivity at all, any so-called subject, and with that would be the absence of objects, too, for they would disappear as "objects." There would be represented a one-way or asymmetrical ontological-material dependence of thought and subjectivity upon its prior contingent non-being. Whatever existence evidenced would be an existence of absolute matter *devoid of* any being which resulted from it. Second, we are able to rationally possess the concept of our non-existence *after our extinction*. If one is able to know that there will be a world continuing after one dies, they are able to in effect conceive of reality devoid of their own subjectivity, uncorrelated, by attaining that state of death even through thought. This is possible by considering the reality or fact of one's own personal death or annihilation in the future (indeed, it is possible, as Brassier does, to imagine a *total* absence of life in the universe come the eventual death of the universe itself in the future).

The trick here is that Meillassoux does not *reject* the correlation: he demonstrates that *it is contingent*, and necessarily so, and attains the unthought *from within it*. It is then possible to attain the face of a form of absolutely necessary contingent existence—an indifferent material cosmos and the necessary contingency of all subjects and objects in it—by looking to the correlation itself rather than either pole taken to be constitutive of its coupling relation. If the contingency of the correlation were not absolute, not necessary, then the correlation would fall prey to a meta-level perspectivalist critique ("I am still *thinking* of my own death, so my own death is just a thought"). But one must readily accept that the fact of one's own non-being, their non-existence, and how that fact does not depend upon their thinking it *to be*. In other words, even the correlationist must admit that the fact that one is contingent necessarily does not depend upon their thinking that they are contingent for it to be. So in essence the claim that "The absolute is the absolutely contingent nature of everything, including the correlation *itself*," must *itself not be contingent at a meta-level*. (As an aside I would interpret this meta-level as a form of "groundless ground"—e.g., Schellingean *Abgrund*—or even indeed as a transcendental condition—one that is *materialist* in its character albeit transcendental nonetheless and hence a "transcendental materialism"). If contingency in this sense means "without reason," then the only principle of reason that there can be is that all things are "without reason," save for the principle itself. In other words, there is no reason that things must be the way that they are—they are contingent and can be otherwise than what they are (non-being), and that is the only necessary principle. As Brassier explains,

> It is worthwhile pausing here to underline the decisive distinction between the idealist and realist variants of the speculative overcoming of correlationism. Speculative idealism claims that the in-itself is not some transcendent

object standing "outside" the correlation, but is rather nothing other than the correlation as such. Thus it converts relationality per se into a thing-in-itself or absolute: the dialectician claims that we overcome the metaphysical reification of the in-itself when we realize that what we took to be merely for-us is in fact in-itself. Correlation is absolutized when it becomes in itself for itself. But this involves transforming correlation into a metaphysically necessary entity or causa sui. By way of contrast, Meillassoux's speculative materialism asserts that the only way to preserve the in-itself from its idealist incorporation into the for-us without reifying it metaphysically is by realizing that what is in-itself is the contingency of the for-us, not its necessity. Thus, when facticity is absolutized, it is the contingency or groundlessness of the for-us (the correlation) which becomes in-itself or necessary precisely insofar as its contingency is not something which is merely for-us. Speculative materialism asserts that, in order to maintain our ignorance of the necessity of correlation, we have to know that its contingency is necessary. In other words, if we can never know the necessity of anything, this is not because necessity is unknowable but because we know that only contingency necessarily exists. What is absolute is the fact that everything is necessarily contingent or "without-reason."

Here we see how if the contingency of the correlation itself is absolutized, made necessarily contingent, then we have grounds to say that by principle all things are contingent (necessarily)—including the correlation. This would allow the correlation to drop away (being contingent) and allow one to speculatively think of reality without subjectivity and as non-correlated, what Meillassoux refers to in his absolute or speculative materialism as the "ancestral" realm. The ancestral realm is, as Meillassoux explains, "any material reality anterior or prior to the emergence of the human species or every recognized form of life on earth."[22] To speak of the ancestral realm is to speak of, describe, a world preceding human consciousness, anterior to any *relation* to the perception of human beings and human consciousness, anterior of the relation of thought to being. The ancestral and its "arche-fossil" are "any beings whose being we cannot conceive of any way other than it is." They indicate not merely as material objects but also as events the existence of any ancestrality prior to any life whatsoever.[23]

In speaking of ancestrality we may now move on to discuss Meillassoux's materialism in connection to his realism. This introduces the final piece of the puzzle in Meillassoux's confrontation with correlationism where it may be demonstrated that for Meillassoux, as for Brassier and Grant, in the new metaphysics materialism and realism complement the aims and goals of the other.

3.4 Mathematics Attaining the Unthought

In *After Finitude* Meillassoux uses postmodern correlationism's denial of the truth of ancestrality—the denial of the truth of the material autonomy which precedes human consciousness—as a test case for his own speculative or absolute materialism and realism. Meillassoux explains that by submitting the ancestral or "archefossil" to the primordial *relatedness* of human perception to whatever it knows or intends as a so-called "truth" or "fact," the correlationist challenges the *non-relative* or *non-correlated* nature of any form of being or truth, even being *prior* to the very emergence of human consciousness knowing it as such. The correlationist claims that human subjectivity can never truly attain perfectly "objective" truth or knowledge, for the meaning of ancestral statements must always be known by a *knower* in order to possess any form of meaning as "objective" or "prior to" the subject they seek to transcend in purported truth. Non-correlated claims of ancestrality are always thus *relative* as a supposed truth or fact "given," known *as* a truth or fact by a subject apprehending it. In this way the subject is the interpretational link between ancestral event-as-fact (always a fact "for us") and anything unknowable prior to the existence of the subject. Or as Nietzsche would rather famously put it, "There are no facts, only interpretations."

For example, for the correlationist the fact that life originated on the earth 3.5 billion years ago becomes a mere statement "Life originated on the earth 3.5 billion years ago for-us." For the correlationist there is always a specific degree of *relativity* of scientific statements in that the *meaning* of scientific statements must be determined being anterior to the givenness of that meaning. Ancestral being must be acknowledged as having some element of givenness so as to be meaningful; which is to say that truth, factuality, objectivity, must always be "given" *for* some observer to take on an independent status of meaning or truth that it is claimed to have. Or, only because human beings and human consciousness now do exist is it possible to "see as a fact" that life originated 3.5 billion years ago. And only because human consciousness uses scientific instruments as essential interpretational devices in the reading and knowing of that data can we say that there is any "fact" present to begin with. Human consciousness must perceive and relate to it so.

Meillassoux explicitly denies even minimal relativity of postmodern theory-ladenness in favor of scientific fact. The "arche-fact" or ancestrality, as he has demonstrated, shows unequivocally the *contingency* of the perceiver where ancestral truth does not depend upon the correlated human being for its being in any way whatsoever. Whether or not human consciousness, the arche-fossil nevertheless shows as fact that life originated at x time where that event itself is asymmetrically independent both causally and ontologically of the human individual knowing or perceiving it as a "fact."

Here, the subjectalist rejoinder is the last straw that a correlationist might try to grab: "To be is to be perceived" as Bishop Berkeley said. But, Meillassoux points out "the sheer lunacy" found in the idea that the factuality of an ancestral statement *depends upon the knower for its veracity* as its true objectivity only becomes more apparent when we consider the asymmetrical nature of its factuality. In other words, had it not been a fact independent of the knower that life originated at x time then there *would be no life to later know it as a fact*. The correlationist at this point cannot draw into their own circle of relative thought events which preceded the very existence of that correlational circle of thought. Doing so only asserts the fact's *independence*, not its *dependence*. We may say, then, that "the fact remains." Ancestrality's ontological independence means also that ancestral events are no more dependent upon their observation for their being than is one's death dependent upon one's thinking about their death in order to be dead.

"How are we to conceive of the empirical sciences' capacity to yield knowledge of the ancestral realm?"[24] For Meillassoux, and following Badiou, *mathematics* is capable of thought thinking being without thought. What is at stake is not only the materialism of Meillassoux's philosophy but his realism. For only under mathematical form is it possible to describe being where humanity is absent, "a world crammed with things and events that are not the correlates of any manifestation; a world that is not the correlate of a relation to the 'world.'"[25] Paradoxically, scientific discourse which is mathematical can manifest being's anteriority to any manifestation. (This is particularly interesting where, for example, Iain Hamilton Grant is interested in the so-called Hubble Problem: we are able to look at telescopic images of an ancient universe before human beings were existing in that universe). This paradox however is only apparent as we shall see, for to think science's "ancestral reach" is to explain *what* exactly mathematics attains.

Subjectalism, other than idealism, is methodologically most susceptible to reading subjective human traits into reality when it collapses *experiential* qualities into what otherwise is devoid of subjectivity itself. In particular, Husserlian transcendental phenomenology collapses the conditions of our knowing the object *into* the object such that the object conforms not only to those conditions of knowing but the manner in which those conditions present the object as appearance. This is to say that conscious experience impugns the object with felt-as intentional qualities taken to be of or in the object itself. The way things are experienced is said to be just the way things are in-themselves. The so-called "givenness" of the object—how that object is in-itself, so says the phenomenologist, is precisely how it is *given to me*. Picking up from Kant's transcendental idealism Husserl collapses the noumenal into the phenomenal, being into thought, within his transcendental phenomenology. Meillassoux refutes the experiential component of any object's givenness however, citing the contingency of the subject and indeed the givenness of those qualities' presentation *to consciousness*.

Meillassoux draws upon the modern distinction between primary and secondary qualities in order to address this problem, stating that secondary qualities are "not in the things themselves."[26] The qualitative experience of *how* something is phenomenologically given is thus inessential to the actual or real properties of the thing itself as it is *apart from me*. As Meillassoux claims, phenomenology has "glorified" subjective apprehension, or "Sensibility is a relation rather than a property in the thing."[27]

Primary qualities, or better, primary properties, on the other hand, are inseparable from the object and belong to the thing even without a consciousness experiencing those properties. For Descartes, for example, these properties pertain to *extension* and therefore are not only compatible terms of a materialist metaphysics (body), but may thus also be subject to *geometrical-mathematical proof*. Meillassoux therefore seeks to "reactivate the Cartesian thesis in contemporary terms": mathematical metaphysics as speculative tool to describe material bodies in terms of length, width, figure, etc. This is to say that anything in mathematical terms can be meaningfully conceived as part of the object itself, "as it is without me." We must, in this way, says Meillassoux, be "resolutely pre-critical."[28]

Meillassoux's appeal to the mathematical via extension reinforces his view about the materiality of bodies and how that materiality does not depend upon human consciousness for its being. Phenomenological subjectalism sunders pretenses to absolute materialism's aspirations toward the objectivity of materiality by relativizing mathematical abstraction to the operations and activities of human consciousness and thought. In particular, although Husserl for example was a mathematician, his *Logical Investigations* (1900/1901) *psychologizes* mathematical description by locating the functional activity of mathematical description in the temporal activity of internal time consciousness. From Husserl's transcendental-idealist perspective the reality of objects involves the reality of consciousness being directed and aware of them in temporal, experiential-apprehension. How one is conscious of objects, including the "felt" manner of their appearance within consciousness, is simply how objects are in themselves.

Moreover, Husserl's transcendental phenomenology requires that whatever consciousness is its contents are *nothing but* a matter of appearances. In other words, by collapsing the noumenal into the phenomenal, the question of whether *there can be* objects apart from their presentation to consciousness is non-important. In his doctrine of intentionality for example, to be conscious is to be *directed* toward some thing, the contents of consciousness. But because of the bracketing involved in the phenomenological method the reality of the contents of consciousness does not arise as a philosophical problem—indeed Husserl, as well as Kant and Heidegger—saw it as a "scandal" that philosophy would ever bother with the problem of whether or how there may be a world absolutely independent of the appearances to consciousness. To be conscious is to be conscious *of* some thing. And human consciousness is always consciousness of something in some way if one is said to be conscious. As part of the bracketing of the phenomenological method the question of reality was stripped away with Husserl's pretense of making phenomenology a rigorous, presuppositionless science. Along with any presuppositions the question of the real, apart from "real-as-conscious-appearance," was rendered null.

Husserl intended phenomenology to be a rigorous, presuppositionless science. Followers of phenomenology questioned whether and to what extent human existence can be understood *without* suppositions or understood in any strictly "neutral" terms. Heidegger for example called into question *Dasein*'s historicity and hoped to lay bare the historical prejudices that the phenomenologist brought to the table. Still others, such as Gadamer or Ricoeur, thought this historical prejudice was ineliminable and indeed was productively constitutive of the interpretations we may take over phenomena. The existential and hermeneutic phenomenologists sought the invariant structures of human existence and consciousness, as well as any historical structures within which phenomena might appear. For Husserl, the beginning point and invariant structure was that of a transcendental Ego, much like Kant whose synthesizing unity of apperception transcendentally anchored any phenomenal appearance within the structures of that synthesizing activity.

Meillassoux sees Husserl's collapse of phenomena and noumena as a strong correlationism and as a subjectalism insofar as sensible qualities of human experience are claimed to be part of the things themselves rather than part of the appropriating process of those things. When the phenomenologist claims that one transcends forward or deeper into the world by focusing on the experiential qualities of an appearance, the further the phenomenologist bores into mere conscious appearance. One never truly steps outside of the transparent cage of consciousness. So while the phenomenologist insists on the independent nature of the appearances the appearances are always *for* consciousness—their reality is always as they are *experientially described*. Reality is always reality-appearing. Thus, reality is always *conditioned*, which was the problem with Kantian finitude and Nietzschean perspectival appearance.

To say as much as I have this far about phenomenology does not mean that phenomenology is always and necessarily an idealism or anti-realism however. Given the distinctions made above between epistemological and metaphysical idealism versus epistemological and metaphysical realism, and the fact that, indeed, the metaphysical realist is often an epistemological idealist, the key point in Meillassoux turning to mathematics as speculative tool involves how mathematics is capable of transcending an experiential correlate with sensible qualities as felt or experienced by consciousness. The transcendental phenomenologist sees these sensible qualities as "real" and as part of the "essence" of whatever is being described. Meillassoux believes that sensible qualities as-felt or as-perceived belong to the subjective pole of the correlation relating to its object as "other." And so we must ask if sensible qualities cannot be a part of the world without the human because their experiential quality is found within consciousness, or whether the sensible is capable of belonging to the real as either a power or property-in-potential that is part of the object itself. If, however, the phenomenologist again states that the way things appear *is* the world and that we indeed can be a phenomenological realist by transcending more deeply "into" the world, we have not answered the question as to whether sensible qualities exist apart from a human consciousness experiencing them.

Tom Sparrow, in his *The End of Phenomenology: Metaphysics and the New Realism* clarifies this point when he explains how there is a sense in which phenomenology appears to "transcend the correlate on its own" by describing *the world*.[29] Whether Heideggerean *ek-stasis* or Sartre's calling out of how phenomenology is an "exploding" toward the world, or Merleau-Ponty referring to the world as "the movement of transcendence"—none of such appears to get to the real because the motion remains within Meillassoux's "transparent cage of consciousness." Meillassoux retorts that for phenomenology, "there is a world only insofar as consciousness transcends itself towards it. Consequently, this space of exteriority is merely the space of what faces us, of what exists only as a correlate of our own existence. This is why, in actuality, we do not transcend ourselves very much by plunging into such a world, for all we are doing is exploring the two faces of what remains a face to face—like a coin which only knows its own obverse."[30]

In this way phenomenology, relating back to Kant's philosophy of a subject-at-center metaphysics, is finitized for as much as it appears to reach into the infinite "rich elsewhere" and its "depths of experience," but Being nevertheless is what *appears* for subjects. Again, though, we must be careful to state that not all phenomenologists state that Being can only exist *because* of subjects. We must be careful to articulate how not all of phenomenology is as idealist as Husserl's transcendental phenomenology was, and that not all of phenomenology somehow necessarily forecloses metaphysical realism, as Sparrow unconvincingly argues. This is simply because we need not take phenomenology to be first and foremost "descriptive reportage" of first-person conscious experience; that is, of a finite subject-at-center philosophy which describes *human experience* always. Here Sparrow seems to fall prey to a simple error in logic that sees all of phenomenologists as idealists and all of phenomenology by its very definition as correlationalist and anti-realist.

As Dan Zahavi has rightly pointed out, the fact that within phenomenology a kind of "transgressive realism" is possible means that, at the very least, other than a realism concerning Husserlian or Platonic essences, phenomenological realism could concern the *autonomy* of reality uncorrelated—for "experience entering our awareness not through pathways prepared by our Active Minds but in spite of them." And it is the alien source of these pathways that, on some accounts, need not phenomenologically involve the distinction of being and thought or correlated consciousness and the appearance-to-consciousness in order to operate. This is to say that Sparrow, and for the most part Meillassoux, take phenomenology to be synonymous with the Husserlian transcendental-idealist variety of that discipline. But I would ask, what of the pre-objective or "pre-thinkable" being discussed within the phenomenologies of Merleau-Ponty or Friedrich Schelling? Is it not the case that in Schelling, Mearleau-Ponty (his late philosophy of nature), but also in Whitehead or C.S. Peirce for example, that the goal for thinking is to turn from nature as it is "for us" or even "before us" to nature thought *from within the perspective of nature itself*? Neither an idealism or realism *sensu stricto*, the Schellingean-Pontyean phenomenology of nature or Peircean mathematical speculative phenomenology of categories positively recognizes an alien pre-reflexive being before the divisions of being and thought: what Schelling called "Identity" or Peirce "Firstness," the absolute uncorrelated. According to Wirth, both Schelling and Ponty (but also Whitehead and Peirce by extension) "sought a way to think the fundamental indivision from nature, the life that is 'already there' *before* the advent of reflection," *before* the bifurcation of subject and object or any thought and being that could be correlated [emphases mine].[31] It seems the more serious charge comes from Meillassoux that phenomenology is *inherently* co-relational and therefore could not be part of a speculative enterprise. But my point here has only been to show that on some accounts phenomenology's descriptive acts are not those which pertain to experiential renderings of appearance, but can, rather, apply to a reality or nature utterly alien to and independent of any appearance much in the same way that Meillassoux's own argument concerning correlationism does. And it does seem that Meillassoux would allow phenomenology to be appropriated as a speculative, mathematical natural science in the service not of speculative description of qualities but of speculative explanation of arche-fact whose results do not reference the sensible secondary qualities of phenomena but rather the powers of pre-reflective phenomena to create, appear, or destroy the consciousness which apprehend them. This would in effect net the same effect of breaking with the correlation.

Meillassoux's rejoinder to the phenomenological position regarding the experiential nature of objects possessing secondary sensible qualities, as described above, was to "break" with the correlation. To break with the correlation is to maintain the independent existence of primary qualities—qualities which are not dependent upon human consciousness for their being. For Meillassoux, in claiming to attain the meaning of mathematical data and information about the universe anterior to human consciousness we are in effect escaping any mode of relation to the properties of conscious human experience. As Meillassoux writes, "Statements are ideal insofar as their reality is one of signification."[32] This does not mean in a Pythagorean way that the universe is *inherently* ideal or mathematical but only that the material reality described by mathematics transcends our experiential consciousness of secondary properties. Through the ontological reach of mathematics we can "get outside of ourselves to grasp the in-itself."[33] Mathematical science and mathematical conceptualization severs the co-existing link between being and manifestation where for transcendental phenomenology being *is* manifestation. By using mathematics and a corresponding absolute materialist ontology thought is in a position to think manifestation's emergence in being as well as true being anterior to manifestation and prior to any appearance. Meillassoux writes that, "there is no fundamental episode in philosophy since Plato that has not proceeded via a re-interpretation of its originary alliance with mathematics," and "what is mathematizable cannot be reduced to a correlate of thought."[34] And, "All of those aspects of the given that are mathematically describable can continue to exist regardless of whether or not we are there to convert the latter into something that is given-to our manifested-for such that things in-themselves are opened up by speculation with mathematical natural science at its side. What we find is that nature becomes exhaustively mathematizable."[35] Through mathematical science "thought has become able to think a world that can dispense with thought, a world that is essentially unaffected by whether or not anyone thinks it."[36]

With Meillassoux's engagement of correlation and his subsequent emphasis on the power of science, in particular mathematical science, to develop a speculative absolutist materialism, the very meaning of how humans are to understand their place in the cosmos has been transformed. Especially opposed to the sort of finitude as introduced by Kant, indeed Meillassoux has transported thought *after* finitude by engaging in a mathematical ontology of the real which nevertheless affirms a material being *devoid* of subjectivity. While Meillassoux rejects the subjectalism (idealism) of Hegel he comes close to Hegel in many other respects including the speculative methodology of "infinite" thought. But unlike Hegel who absolutizes the correlation in necessity Meillassoux absolutizes the necessary *contingency* of the correlation and indeed all else. Still, Meillassoux's realism, materialism, and metaphysics is pre-critical and in his own words "bizarrely classical." As it stands and given that Meillassoux has claimed that Hegel is his "secret master," the relationship between Meillassoux's speculative project and that of Hegel remains largely unexplored. As John Caputo has pointed out, there is a certain respect in that reading the two side by side demonstrates how the meaning of their ontologies up until a certain point is indistinguishable. Still further, Meillassoux's eschatological ontology of the creation of worlds, his thought on the dead and justice, the divine inexistence, his "figures" of factiality, his neo-rationalism, all invite further comparison and study of his own philosophy with respect to that of Hegel. Far from looking upon Hegel as some sort of simple Absolute Idealist or as representing the ultimate form of subjectalist correlationism, Meillassoux's philosophy is indebted to Hegel more than most probably realize. Hegel's phenomenology understood as the science of the experience of consciousness and his dazzling speculative logic as presented in the *Science of Logic and the Phenomenology of Spirit* seems to be of the utmost importance for Meillassoux's theory of the advent and creation of worlds, his thoughts concerning necessity, facticity, and contingency. This is especially true of Meillassoux's philosophical theology that emphasizes the possibility of divine incarnation to bring about the Fourth World of Justice. Indeed if I were to venture a guess I would say that if one wishes to comprehend fully what Meillassoux's philosophy of the absolute entails, one *cannot* do so unless one has seriously studied Hegel.

The time has come to leave aside Meillassoux as our first and predominant emblematic philosopher of the speculative turn. My hope has been to show how, acting against the currents of 20th-century anti-absolutist philosophy Meillassoux's call for open speculation and metaphysical philosophy has indeed been a radical call worthy of attention. There is much more that could be said of Meillassoux's ontology (especially with respect to phenomenology, although I cannot spend more time addressing those avenues here). My goal here has been to simply point to the most significant moments within Meillassoux's realist, materialist, metaphysics found in *After Finitude* so that we might see how his philosophical daring has influenced so many others.

In his efforts to absolutize thought in order to attain what is unthought, that is what is outside of thought ("the great outdoors," the real devoid subjectivity, i.e., from the standpoint of "absolute materialism"), two other philosophers are similar to Meillassoux in that their own realist, materialist metaphysics reconceive being, nature, and reality in ways that have speculatively challenged the orthodoxies of Continental philosophy described in the second chapter of this book. These two other philosophers are Ray Brassier and Iain Hamilton Grant. Whereas Meillassoux has taken Continental philosophy "after" Kantian finitude both Brassier and Grant push Continental thinking past traditionally conceived limits in terms of how it thinks "after" nature. However, this is not to say that either Brassier or Grant do not reject Kantian finitude. They do. But each proceeds "after" finitude by turning to a philosophy of nature, or a kind of naturalism, that Meillassoux does not. Moreover, both Brassier and Grant understand "materialism" in a very different sense than Meillassoux, and each in their own way. Thus it is even more important to determine as to how both

Brassier and Grant understand "nature." It is to the work of Brassier and Grant that this text now turns.

Resources for Further Reading

Gratton, Peter, and Paul Ennis, eds., *The Meillassoux Dictionary* (Edinburgh: Edinburgh University Press, 2014).

Meillassoux, Quentin, *After Finitude*, translated by Raymond Brassier with a Foreword by Alain Badiou (London: Continuum, 2008).

Meillassoux, Quentin, "From 'l'inexistence divine,'" translated by Nathan Brown, *Parrhesia* Vol. 25 (2016): 20–40: http://www.parrhesiajournal.org/parrhesia25/parrhesia25_meillassoux.pdf.

Meillassoux, Quentin, interviewed by Florian Hecker and Robin Mackay, "Speculative Solution: Quentin Meillassoux and Florian Hecker Talk Hyperchaos." *Urbanomic* July 22, 2010: https://www.urbanomic.com/document/speculative-solution-meillassoux-hecker/.

Meillassoux, Quentin, "There Is Contingent Being Independent of Us, and This Contingent Being Has No Reason to Be of a Subjective Nature: Interview with Quentin Meillassoux." In *New Materialism: Interviews & Cartographies*, edited by Rick Dolphijn and Iris van der Tuin (Ann Arbor: Open Humanities Press, 2012): https://quod.lib.umich.edu/o/ohp/11515701.0001.001/1:4.4/--new-materialism-interviews-cartographies?rgn=div2;view=fulltext.

Zahavi, Dan, "The End of What? Phenomenology vs. Speculative Realism." *International Journal of Philosophical Studies* Vol. 24, No. 3 (2016): 289–309: https://www.academia.edu/25503083/The_end_of_what_Phenomenology_vs_speculative_realism.

Notes

1. Meillassoux, *After Finitude*, 27.
2. Meillassoux, *After Finitude*, 29.
3. Meillassoux, *After Finitude*, 28.
4. Meillassoux, *Philosophy in the Making*, 170.
5. Meillassoux, *Philosophy in the Making*, 170–171.
6. Meillassoux, *After Finitude*, 13.
7. Meillassoux, *After Finitude*, 7.
8. Meillassoux, *After Finitude*, 14.
9. Meillassoux, *After Finitude*, 21.
10. Cf. Hegel's *Phenomenology of Spirit*, "Force and the Understanding."
11. Meillassoux, "Time without Becoming."
12. Meillassoux, *After Finitude*, 35.
13. Brassier, *Nihil Unbound*, 65.
14. Brassier, *Nihil Unbound*, 65.
15. Brassier, *Nihil Unbound*, 65.
16. Meillassoux, *After Finitude*, 36.
17. Meillassoux, *After Finitude*, 37.
18. Meillassoux, *After Finitude*, 37.
19. Meillassoux, "Time without Becoming."
20. See Meillassoux, "Time without Becoming."
21. Meillassoux: *Philosophy in the Making*, Interview.

22 Meillassoux, *After Finitude*, 10.
23 Meillassoux, *After Finitude*, 22.
24 Meillassoux, *After Finitude*, 47.
25 Meillassoux, *After Finitude*, 47.
26 Meillassoux, *After Finitude*, 2.
27 Meillassoux, *After Finitude*, 2.
28 Meillassoux, *After Finitude*, 3.
29 Sparrow, *The End of Phenomenology*, 93.
30 Meillassoux, *After Finitude*, 6.
31 Wirth, "Editor's Introduction," in *The Barbarian Principle*.
32 Meillassoux, *After Finitude*, 12.
33 Meillassoux, *After Finitude*, 27.
34 Meillassoux, *After Finitude*, 103, 117.
35 Meillassoux, *After Finitude*, 115.
36 Meillassoux, *After Finitude*, 116. It is crucial to note that the mathematically-compatible-with-reality ontologies of C.S. Peirce, Alfred North Whitehead, and while themselves not mathematicians—Merleau-Ponty or Friedrich Schelling—all present secret but hitherto unopened doors to the "Great Outdoors" in non-correlationist fashion. Even Hegel, if constructively re-retrieved, can offer quite powerfully tools for a speculative, realist phenomenology.

IV
After Nature

4.1 Speculative Nihilism/Transcendental Realism in *Nihil Unbound*

BRASSIER'S SPECULATIVE NIHILISM/TRANSCENDENTAL realism and Grant's speculative idealism/transcendental materialism each have their affinities with Meillassoux's open call for speculation yet both turn directly to *nature* as a main domain of inquiry within their own respective speculative projects. And similar to each is their reliance upon the choice to refuse the Kantian philosophy of subject-at-center and its corresponding ontological finitude and proceed instead to follow the German idealists in the infinitizing of thought; that is, in speculating what thought is capable of attaining other than its own strict phenomenological subjectivity (Brassier by course of Hegel as picked up in the work of Brandom and Sellars, and Grant through Schelling). As

Sellars and Schelling both accept the reconciliation of realism and idealism, or better, nature and concept, not only are Grant and Brassier speculative philosophers, they are realists *insofar as* they are *transcendental naturalists* where the distinction between the two may be parsed out between Brassier's *transcendental realism* and Grant's *transcendental materialism.* Thus, the meaning of these terms should be made clear.

First, "transcendental naturalism," according to Brassier, "Seeks to identify the general features that any conceptual system must possess in order to know the nature of which it is a part."[1] A "transcendental materialism," is, as Grant explains following Schelling, "empiricism extended to the Absolute." And "transcendental realism" seeks to adjudicate between the *conditions* of thinking and the *autonomy* of thinking, thus *locating* rationality and its conceptual agency within nature. Or, as Grant expresses, the Schellingean project of "the *unconditioning* of the metaphysics of nature."[2] For each the question is how the conceptual partakes of nature or *is* nature and yet is so without itself *conditioning* or *grounding* any real knowledge of nature, of which it is a part. There is thus a tension between thought and being (pace Meillassoux) that finds its expression as a tension between rational concept and sensible nature as well as the conditions for conceptuality as such.

As Brassier notes, and here let me reproduce the whole quote simply because of its importance regarding *how* he understands the relationship between realism, materialism, and metaphysics—particularly with respect to Hegel,

I consider myself an idealist, opposed to a materialist, as I insist on the need to preserve the relative autonomy of thinking, and the cogency and the consistency of thinking, and of conceptual rationality, precisely in order to be able to adjudicate the relationship between thinking and reality, between theory and practice, and also it's an enabling condition for practice. In other words, if you try to fuse thought into material reality indiscriminately, I think that leads to an impotent short-circuit. So I would insist on defending the representational structures that are simply attacked [...] it's a caricature of representation that's being attacked, it's a straw man. Representation here, and theoretical representation in particular, is a straw man.

I want to defend the imperatives of conceptualization, and even a kind of dialectics, as although I agree with what Nick [Land] says about the way in which death is a marker for real identity of matter itself, the point is that you should never confuse the symbolic marker for the thing in itself. You need a much more careful and subtle articulation of those terms—actually, between zero, one, and two—to explain the autonomy of thought and rationality and of thinking. Not to put too fine a point on it, so that you can maintain and generate a locus of rational agency. In other words, keep a space of subjectivation open that provides a prism for practical incision, a point of insertion. And that has to be done, and I think this involves re-examining the legacy of Hegel, and of Hegelianism. In other words, to maintain a kind of conceptual rationality that necessitates transformation at the level of practical existence. It requires a lot of theoretical work to do this. I would insist on the need to preserve the autonomy of rationality as something that allows you to intervene, to cut, in the continuity.[3]

The manner in which Brassier fuses thought into matter discriminately is to use thought's capacity to conceptualize its own absence. This in turn shows how we need not think that because thought or concepts belong to reality that reality is itself thoroughly conceptual. Indeed this argumentative procedure by way of thought experiment as confirmed by science is echoed by Meillassoux's appeal to the scientifically verifiable, yet mathematically describable, ancestral realm. Brassier takes us in the other direction and points to thought's inevitable extinction in order to sever the dependence of being upon thought. This was the major task of his book *Nihil Unbound*.

It should be stated that the project begun in that book has transformed considerably since its publication. So much so that in a relatively recent interview Brassier has maintained that the book is a "botched job."[4] Whereas before a concern with humanity's enlightenment to extinction within ontological register preoccupied

Brassier early in his career, he has since turned from the speculative nihilism of *Nihil Unbound* to a still-developing transcendental realism by way of further elucidating the relationship between naturalism and rationality within the framework of a Sellarsian scientific-realist metaphysics (which also did figure in *Nihil Unbound* but which has figured even more prominently in his work since). It is for these reasons I will focus not on *Nihil Unbound* but on statements of Brassier's philosophy since.

As Brassier makes clear, Sellars proposes a distinction between the "scientific" and "manifest" image. On the one hand, the manifest image is the image of human-self within philosophical reflection; and on the other hand, the scientific image is the image of human-self within "complex physical system"—one "distilled" from various scientific discourses, whether physics, neuro-physiology, or evolutionary biology.[5] For our purposes here it is worth noting immediately that Brassier's realism and materialism is not necessarily *reductively* physicalist as many suppose, for reasons we shall elaborate upon in a moment. But the point is worth mentioning simply due to the fact that many have charged Sellars with similar criticism: that his *naturalism is naively scientific or physicalist and hence reductionistic*. But such could not be further from the truth. While it is true that Brassier has a healthy respect for the sciences and is much interested in cognitive science (what today many would paint as an "eliminative materialism") we must respect that the positioning of his philosophy "after" philosophies of nature which have included folk-psychological aspects of human consciousness and normativity within them (but also normative theories attempting to anchor *intrinsic* meaning and purpose within the conceptual activities of organisms) is a positioning that takes place vis-à-vis a sophisticated re-articulation of *metaphysical rationalism*; e.g., the same sort of *idealism* that Iain Grant re-articulates in similar materialist-realist, speculative register. In that sense Hegel and Kant are as important interlocutors for his philosophy as Sellars is.

Turning back to Kant, Brassier's naturalism is at once *rationalist* and *empiricist*, though of course each in different respects. The bridge between each is Sellarsian naturalism in key of *pragmatism*. In short we simply might summarize that the importance of Sellarsian naturalism-as-pragmatism induces opportunity for Brassier to successfully interpret the claims of normativity within the context of his discussions concerning the importance of science: normativity is heavily criticized within *Nihil Unbound* in the context of phenomenology, but not without admitting the reality or importance of *the conceptual*. And the conceptual, if nothing else, secures itself as index for rational agency. Rational agency is important for, as we have seen in the quote above, it means that the activity of reason itself is important for understanding what speculative philosophy is capable of doing when it comes to articulating what thought does when it considers nature, of which it is a part. But the overall point is that by way of Sellars Brassier is through his own work able to justify a kind of rationalism previously inadmissible in post-Kantian Continental philosophy. For where in extant trends of Continental philosophy the concern has been "humans in the world"—here, but now close to ten years after the publication of *Nihil Unbound*—Brassier is able to discuss from a viewpoint amenable to Continental thought "the world" but without the human; this without having to appeal to the speculative nihilist thought experiment which has garnered his philosophy (unfairly) the label of "scientific reductionism." And while Brassier's philosophy of nature is certainly friendly to the sciences it does not reduce its scope to those sciences if only because it does not *limit* its theoretical output to either utility or empirically verifiable phenomena. It embraces activities of conceptualization not immediately present in the data it utilizes for its justification.

A second feature in Brassier's realism, materialism, and metaphysics is his insistence upon the power of the negative (conceptual negativity) within the domain of thinking about nature. In particular one finds in his article "That Which Is Not: Philosophy as Entwinement of Truth and Negativity" him taking a stand against contemporary nominalists who "deny the norm of truth in order to affirm the immanence of being."[6] Brassier turns to two arch-idealists who may be used to reappraise the possible alliance between negativity and materialism: Plato and Hegel. For Brassier, naturalism and materialism are not equivalent and his naturalism certainly does not forbid his drawing upon idealist metaphysics to make his case.

Brassier's thesis is that "anyone wanting to repotentiate the power of the negative against an increasingly complacent 'affirmationist' consensus in contemporary theory—conspicuously exemplified by the resurgence of unabashedly vitalist and pan-psychist metaphysics—will have to reconsider the valence of critiques of conceptual truth (and therefore philosophy, to the extent that philosophy is the discipline of conceptualization [...])."

Let us now turn to Brassier's latest statements in order to allow his philosophy to speak for itself. First, the truth of negativity is a truth beyond force (Nietzsche); one is to not merely salvage the "ideality of truth" from materialism, but should "rehabilitate truth's critical potency" against inane contemporary "materialisms" which are nothing more than relativisms in disguise: nominalisms par excellence. The tension here is between "the materialization of the idea and the idealization of matter."[7] We may turn to Plato, but also to Hegel, to learn to acknowledge the way in which the non-being of the Idea is entwined with the being of matter. That is, thought and being are intertwined conceptually but also via the negative-non-being.

Brassier begins that the "failure to acknowledge [the] entwining of being and otherness erases the difference between essence and appearance, and stymies the rationalist imperative to explain phenomena by penetrating to the reality beyond appearances."[8] Brassier states that in this context the contemporary and much-celebrated Continental philosopher, Bruno Latour, is among the guilty of reducing reason to mere discrimination in order to salvage the reality of every appearance, "from sunsets to Santa Claus."[9] Latour reduces the rationality of science to mere "force," but loses the actual force of *conceptualization* found in Nietzsche's own critique. For Latour, scientific knowledge is reduced to practical "know how," and truth is reduced to "mere" power. Contemporary nominalist "materialisms" reduce reason, science, and knowledge—truth—to arbitration, custom, manipulation, propaganda, affect, force. In a series of allusive metaphors, "actor," "ally," "force," "power," "strength," "resistance," and "network" supplement the conceptual and cognitive behind every actor, something that an entire philosophical tradition from Plato to Sellars has taken to be a problematic.[10] As one can see, this positions Brassier as being emblematic of the realist yet speculative philosophers who directly challenge the subject-at-center metaphysics of Kant and subjectalist metaphysics of contemporary Continental thought. For Brassier, Latour signifies subjectalism.

Brassier continues his attack upon Latour's subjectalism, by writing, "Philosophical theory is not a matter of explicating the socio-linguistic conditions of explicitation but is to discover their formal infrastructure found within thinking and its conceptual practice, to "set out the preconditions for knowing how to think and to speak [...] The explicit representation of latent representational mechanisms."[11] Brassier's aim is to "extract the common core of signification presupposed by immediacy and its immediate negation. This is, of course, a reworking of Hegel's account of mind's coming to self-consciousness [...] Philosophy is the explicitation of truth, understood as the formal manifestation of latent content carried out via the representation of representation."[12]

There can be no transcendent critique of reason, for "critique is a normative term whose ultimate warrant derives from reason itself."[13] Following Brandom, "The reconstruction of Hegel's account of the self-correcting character of rationality is to demonstrate that a commitment to the uncircumventable authority of conceptuality need not entail the metaphysical hypostasis of reason as some sort of supernatural faculty. [This is neither] a warrant for those varieties of irrationalism that claim to contest its [reason's] legitimacy in the name of some allegedly a-rational experience or force" ala Nietzsche or Bergson.

In sum, for Brassier "the transcendental difference between appearance and reality indexes a form of negativity that is at once the condition of objective truth in discourse, but also is that which cannot be objectified without undermining the possibility of such truth. This negativity does not index a difference between recognizable 'thing's or entities but a unilateral distinction between the structure of objectifying discourse and its unobjectifiable motor: the non-being of the real as an irreducible remainder [...] This nothingness provides the ultimate source of the non-conceptual negativity that fuels dialectical negativity (i.e. the negation of the concept)." Practices anchor one to an extraconceptual order, so this is why the rejection of the myth of the given does not lead one to suppose that reality is just a linguistic construct (traditional nominalism) but rather to suppose that language (as a practice) is embedded in non-linguistic yet conceptually and dialectically functioning reality. A reality-without-human yet which is itself rational and potent by way of dialectical negativity, what places Brassier in a unique way next to Hegel. Both admit the asubjective rational, conceptual character of the Absolute which is no mere congruence of plural perspectives competing for power. It is, rather, incessant indifferent reality blindly accommodating the irrational into the rational through the various creative processes of conceptual practice. Brassier's naturalism is capacious because processes, though without *meaning*, are robust.

4.2 Speculative Idealism/ Transcendental Materialism in *Philosophies of Nature after Schelling*

In recent years there has been a resurgence of interest in the German idealist Friedrich Wilhelm Joseph von Schelling. Within Continental speculative philosophy especially many have turned to the ranks of German idealism in order to sort out the exact character of the relation between realism, materialism, and metaphysics; or, in this context, between a transcendental philosophy of nature that does not reduce nature to *mere* matter in its reality and reductionist forms of post-Kantian 20th-century Continental philosophy that do not tackle the question of nature at all. Like Brassier, Grant's mission in his 2008 *Philosophies of Nature after Schelling* seeks to know "How does nature come to be thought?" To answer such a question, the meaning of both "nature" and "thought" Grant tells us, must be "overhauled." Grant's metaphysics is one of naturephilosophy: a consideration of the Absolute thought of as nature "originally and necessarily" in its "grounds" and as it "grounds everything that our species has ever thought about nature."[14] The Absolute is unconditioned, now conceived of as "the All"—not as all "things" but the All that *is* all things. Grant's speculative metaphysics is immanentist and "materialist" in that it occurs "within" the Absolute yet also does not seek any "fixed position" outside of it or beyond it, for "after nature" or "beyond nature" is an impossibility if nature is All; this as metaphysical thesis despite in the Aristotelian tradition (which Grant heavily criticizes) where *metaphysics* means "about nature"—*meta* (about) *phusis* (nature). To engage in metaphysics "after" nature means to proceed ontologically "within" nature—in particular from within nature as pure constructing activity. On the other hand, by recognizing nature's own activity of *pure construction* Grant's philosophy is at once materialist as much as it is *transcendental*.

Grant understands nature as the Absolute, following Schelling as "product and productivity" but more fundamentally as "Absolute activity that cannot be exhibited by any finite product."[15] Nature is all that there is, there is nothing that is non-natural or so supernatural that cannot be said to belong to it. Hence there is nothing outside of nature, nor before it, nor even after it. Nature is "absolute activity exhibited ad infinitum."[16] For from where other than within nature's activity could such claim *about* nature be made? This is indeed what makes nature the Absolute (*das Unbedingte*, "the Unconditioned"). Nature is unconditioned precisely because it is always the starting point: there is absolutely nowhere to begin *other* than nature and hence nothing which could be its meaningful opposite. In this way nature is, following Schelling, a *precondition* for thinking. And if nature understood as Absolute is a precondition for thinking thought itself must be part and parcel of the natural, its "medium."[17] And if this is true, we cannot in fact state along with Kant that *thought* grounds nature, for only nature grounds nature—nature must ground itself—if, again, nature precedes thought and its attempt to ground (condition reality). Only nature is the true a priori transcendental, the ground of all that is. This in effect immediately distances Grant's ontology from post-Kantian philosophies that claim reality (nature) is always conditioned rather than itself being the unconditioned condition of whatever is. In short, this is Grant's metaphysical *realism*—one feature that makes his philosophy a particularly good example of the new metaphysics, pace Meillassoux as discussed earlier in this book.

Other than speculating upon the Absolute, albeit in a different manner, Grant is like Meillassoux in a second way. He rejects Kantian finitude because it excises the in-itself from metaphysics and jettisons speculation-as-metaphysics for the epistemological. If the goal is to discover how nature comes to be thought, and thought is not *about* nature but *of* it, then, as Schelling wrote "to philosophize about nature means to create it."[18] Grant claims that the epistemologizing confines of both analytic philosophy but also 20th-century post-Kantian Continental philosophy ignored this fact, and yet 20th-century philosophy overall chose to follow a normative path rather than an ontological one. Epistemology's replacement of metaphysics (or its normativization of metaphysics as epistemology, the *conditioning* of the real by the structures of human language and knowledge) here, then, incapacitates speculative philosophy's attempts to "*make* rather than merely criticize."[19] And according to

Grant both 20th-century Continental philosophy and analytic philosophy have followed Kant in accomplishing that. In short, Grant explains that Schellingean naturephilosophy could lead contemporary philosophy beyond mere representation. This is to be accomplished by teaching us that we ought not turn to Kantian a prior categories of cognition but to follow Schelling in looking to the indwelling and organic *logical form* of nature.

The logical forms of nature according to Grant should not be interpreted as a prioristic in any sense of Kantian transcendentalism, however. The speculative physics in play is one that is also a "materialist empiricism" that "reaches beyond the Kant-inspired critique of metaphysics, its subjectivist-epistemological transcendentalism, and its isolation of physics from metaphysics."[20] Kant's logic of appearance "deposes ontology" whereas the ontological necessity found in the physics of the All—the speculative physics of nature—is established primordially *by nature itself*. Schelling is the philosopher who overthrows the Copernican revolution by engaging nature "beyond simple representation."[21] Here *phusis* defeats a priori the prospect of its *appearance* for any finite phenomenological conscious grasping of it. Because of nature's a priori determination, it establishes rather than emerges within any so-called necessity of "appearance."

Grant takes Schellingean naturephilosophy to uphold these principles but also retrieve ontology even more deeply than Kantian and post-Kantian critical philosophy. Turning to Heidegger (whose concept of Beyng was influenced by Schelling: see Heidegger's *Contributions to Philosophy* for example), Grant states that Heidegger saw in Schelling the notion that nature, or for Heidegger Being (Beyng), is often mistakenly taken by philosophers to mean *beings*—specifically *beings as a whole*. It was Kant who defined nature as "the sum total of *things*" insofar as they are "objects of the senses." For Grant, objects are "a late arrival," and any ontology of "objects" de facto eliminates nature necessarily for nature or Beyng is *noministically* reduced to "existentia est singulorum": the metaphysics of simples. Object-oriented ontology therefore does not investigate *nature itself* but rather only *isolated parts of the world*.[22] Again, this is not to say that nature is a container for things and is not all "things" at all; rather, nature is the All that *is* all things.

The problem of seeing nature as isolated substances, objects, or "things" presents yet another problem. As each individual or singular is subjected to the reductionism of a nominalistic metaphysics, one loses what Badiou has called "the non-logical concept of ground." Schelling re-examines this concept of ground throughout his work insofar as he is interested in what *makes* a subject, rather than articulating the nature of *subjects*. For Grant, the Schellingean thesis that speculative physics ought to encounter "the ungrounding that precedes all ground" (*Abgrund*) so as to regain ontology is a thesis that opposes the Kantian substance-predicate logic inherited from Aristotle, as the Aristotelian logic bypasses the All in favor of individual substances pre-articulated and individuated. In place of that logic of "things" or "beings as entities" Grant's speculative idealism/speculative physics is a *transcendental materialism* through its focus on *the dynamics of ground no longer "grounded in somatism"*—no longer grounded in "things" at all.[23] Matter is "not corporeal"—it is transcendental in its own "dynamic process of construction"—matter as *natura naturans* or "nature naturing" and not *natura naturata* "natured natured." This radicalization of transcendental philosophy is also compatible, so says Grant, with a Platonic "physics of the All": a "Platonic physics"[24] insofar as any individual *becomes* its own being and is not any being *already*. Therefore, Grant's philosophy may also be called a transcendental materialism as much as it is a Platonic physics of things as respective Idea (achievement of Form). This may appear odd at first considering idealism's aversion of matter or appropriation of matter into the ideal. But we are wont to remember that Grant's idealism is *speculative* and that as such it may find a way to account for matter not as irreducibly *physical* but as *dynamic* yet *sensible*.

Here Grant introduces Schelling's "speculative physics" as a way to reach "beyond the Kant-inspired critique of metaphysics, its subjectivist-epistemological transcendentalism, and its isolation of physics from metaphysics."[25] And Grant announces his alternative prospect and goal quite clearly: "Schelling provides a rare instance of the as yet mostly untried consequence of exiting the Kantian framework and rejecting the phenomenal determination of nature, reworking a theory not of the self but of the in-itself. This unconditioning of the construction and use of concepts with regard to the self-construction of matter [...] [is where] [...] conceptual genesis and natural genesis become one."[26] So again, to define our terms, Grant's metaphysics speculatively extends beyond the Kantian cage of epistemological appearance—particularly the appearance of *things* guided by an a priori constructive logic of subject and predicate rendering things as isolated substantial units—and instead establishes a transcendental materialism first and foremost being an empiricism extended to the Absolute. In other words, taken from the other side, his project is also a speculative idealism in its extension beyond Kant for it engages a speculative physics of the Idea as much as it engages the dynamics behind or within the construction of bodies and the mutual ground(s) of generation (constructing activity). We therefore have a materialism that is speculative, and non-paradoxically, an idealism that is empirical for it is a physics of Idea. The lynchpin between the speculatively ideal and materialist-empirical is, quite interestingly, the philosophy of Plato—particularly as Grant picks up Schelling's reading of Plato through the *Timaeus*.

Grant sets out his thesis most clearly in his *Philosophies of Nature after Schelling*, although of course he reifies this thesis in several important articles after. Here however I would like to remain with his 2008 book, for the first chapter on Schelling (which we have summarized so far) and his second chapter on Plato both lead directly to his conclusion drawn in the last chapter of the book. Having discussed Schelling now allow me to discuss how Plato completes the picture of Grant's philosophy, which in essence demonstrates how his philosophy innovatively represents the new metaphysics.

The process begins with Grant's unique appropriation of Plato understood as a one-world theorist through the naturephilosophy of the German idealist Schelling. Noted earlier, to call Plato a one-world theorist is essentially anathema to many Plato scholars who carry on, in the Continental tradition at least, the received interpretation of Plato as two-world-theorist in order to deny Platonic forms of absolutism. But Grant challenges this notion by attending to Schelling's "non-eliminative Idealism" and reading it into a Platonic physics, thereby creating a "Platonic physics of the Idea," a "dynamics of the sensible," or a "physics of the All." In short it is through Schelling (and in a less discussed but equally important way Plato) that nature should become "capable of the Idea."[27] And while Grant, like Brassier and Meillassoux, refuses the making subset of ontology to the normative —his major complaint against 20th-century Continental philosophy—he is also very much unlike his emblematic speculative contemporaries in their criticisms of 20th-century continental thought in his choice to make Fichte and Deleuze his counterpoint.

In the second chapter "The Powers Due to Becoming: The Reemergence of the Platonic Physics in the Genetic Philosophy" as well as conclusion to *Philosophies of Nature after Schelling*, Grant sets out his thesis that Schelling's naturephilosophy finds its best expression as a *genetic* form of philosophy when it develops commentary upon Plato's *Timaeus*. Less than a commentary, Grant believes, Schelling's thinking through of the *Timaeus* is nothing short of a "collaborative ideating" much like Whitehead or Heidegger who in like manner think along with that text rather than articulate a mere narrative in the history of ideas. Grant argues that Schelling utilizes Plato to advance the thesis that the Idea is the "infinite concept," where rather than attaching conditions to the unconditions or "restricting the absolute" the absolute is presented as the generation of the materiality of matter.[28] Against Kant and utilizing a Platonic materialist ontology of the Idea Schelling contests Kantian *eliminativism* seeking to establish "not merely forms of our understanding, but universal world concepts."[29] These universal world concepts function much in the same manner as Meillassoux's "figures" or specific conditions of facticity. In this sense as a form of the universe and not merely the understanding Ideas must include the physical universe and be capable of its ideation or creation.

The physical existence of the Idea becomes philosophical priority Grant tells us most exceptionally through Schelling's engagement with Plato's *Timaeus*. This physical existence beholds matter as *power* and hence a "powers ontology." He writes, "Platonic physics has as its task to explain the 'emergence' or 'coming into being' of this universe" and how it acquires body.[30] The somatics in question is one in which creative genesis is central category. Much the same as, for example, the process-relational philosophy of Alfred North Whitehead or Charles Sanders Peirce, in the words of Schelling, "materiality alone is not yet corporeality."[31] A vital dynamic undergirds any material formation, or conceptual formation. And so Ideas as in the two-world interpretation of Plato are *not* essential or perfect archetypes upon which physical objects are modeled—they are powers afforded by nature. There is a unity therefore of the dynamic and transcendental, vital and material. It is *because* of the nature of the Idea that nature *is* productive.

Again, the devitalization of the Idea is, Grant tells us, due to the twofold "fallacy of misplaced concreteness" (here Grant cites Whitehead) enacted by Aristotle and later by Kant. The epistemologization of the ideal-but-corporeal *generating* nature-ontology of Plato, mostly through the unquestioning acceptance of the Aristotelian substance-predicate logic, in turn ingrained the tendency of any metaphysics to regionalize itself to physics: a specific concept of matter as "concrete thing." In tension with Meillassoux's speculative materialism, Grant does not accept a Democritean or Lucretian account of materiality for he does not accept any substantial unity for strictly pre-individuated material objects. Objects are in Grant's view "late acquisitions." Plato's "secret teaching" is nothing but the materiality of the Idea and how only ideas could be the necessary preconditions for individuation which is always a *process* of achievement rather than mere given. Following Schelling, Grant likewise contends that matter is an *achievement of form* rather than thinking there simply is a "universe of things."[32] The notion that a universe simply could be composed of a "plurality of distinct individual entities" had by perception without recourse to the imperceptible forces of generation or grounds of generation is utterly foreign to the sort of nature ontology that Grant proposes. Because Aristotle's physics is a "shallow range empiricism" it misses the imperceptible by correlating perception (observation) with reality and thereby misses reality's ideal generation.[33]

In other words, Grant believes that Aristotle misses the true nature of matter by focusing on substance and form and not the generative activity of matter itself.

The specific instructions of the speculative physics of the Ideas which, following Plato through Schelling, Grant wishes to carry out, are indeed complex. Suffice it to say however that the powers of generation may be traced intelligible through the Schellingean act of intellectual intuition; that is, through the immediacy of sensible feeling. Brassier likewise draws upon Bergson in Bergson's non-phenomenology prehension of immediate sense experience (as much as Brassier rejects Bergsonian vitalism and the phenomenological feeling "of" feeling). Likewise, the true nature of metaphysics as speculative physics is the transcendental and formal determination via intellectual intuition of matter's specific construction. As *activity* this construction is imperceptible—yet not entirely devoid of sense. Perception becomes ideal in the same manner, for example, that a mathematician or geometer might mentally "construct" an ideal proof. From these constructions one abduces world-concepts or figures that are not representations of any order but are themselves emergences of order. This reconceives the very nature of transcendental philosophy in a Schellingean (if not Peircean or Whiteheadian) key, as categories are not formal representations or even presentations of nature—they are, instead, *modalizations*, nature's own modes of becoming. Ideas thus become prime organizing factors and sources of creation, simultaneously.

4.3 Conclusion

Is the position of a philosophy of nature that is both a naturalism and an idealism a paradox? As Iain Grant writes, "A naturalism regarding reason, for instance, entails that the problem of sufficient cause does not exhaust that of ground, which must also include, at a minimum, ground as causal; yet how does 'nature' resolve this problem? What is the ground of ground?"[34] And furthermore, what is the "nature" of this ground? This is perhaps *the* fundamental question shared by the philosophies of Grant and Brassier, and indeed by those who now can be said to be proceeding "after" the speculative turn: in what way is a transcendental philosophy compatible with a thoroughgoing naturalism? Is a "transcendental naturalism" possible?

It is my goal in a very personal sense to take on in the future as my own project an attempt to answer these questions. In doing so I hope to extend and continue not as a mere commentator, as I have been in the past, but as one who is actively constructing just as much as Meillassoux, Grant, or Brassier, a speculative continuation of the spirit of the new metaphysics within my own systematic although fallible statement. While in the past I have edited books engaging in the question of conscious experience or the "second-order" *products* of the natural world, I have as of yet to engage *the real* within an ontological-speculative "thought operation" per *itself*. And while my first book and several articles very lightly sketched my own viewpoint—which I have called a "speculative naturalism"—I have as of yet to heavily demarcate the outlines and features of where such a sort of naturalism might lead the speculative endeavor.

The key ideas for a "speculative naturalism," realist and materialist in orientation, is that these metaphysical positions are developed so that they are thoroughly *ecological*, that is, capable of accommodating the conceptually laden yet indifferent Absolute which is nature in dialectical process, but also capture the sense of generativity and relationality between the processes of nature (or process) and the *sources* of such generativity and process, namely, the *Ideas*. Thus, speculative naturalism must be an ecological metaphysics as much as it is a realist, speculative, and materialist metaphysics. This requires, I believe, first and foremost a challenge to the previously dominant subject-at-center metaphysics and subjectalist articulation of contemporary phenomenology. The anthropocentric viewpoint of such a metaphysics might be challenged or problematized in two ways.

First, nature is not always beautiful. It can be downright ugly or grotesque as much as it can be sublime and breathtaking. We must represent nature in its full range of value and abandon a certain form of romanticized nature as something utterly conducive to human needs and desires. Nature always has the last vote, and in its sheer scope, complexity, and power demands humility as humans realize they are but one of many actors in a vast network of others. So contrasts of aesthetic value make for a canvass of nature that is as much bleak as it is bright. Brassier first touched upon this in *Nihil Unbound*, but the "depths" of nature are touched upon in Grant's *Philosophies of Nature after Schelling*.

Second, human beings need to rethink how things are related in the world. There is no super-order or container of "Nature." We shouldn't state that nature is just "natured" actors on the stage. We need to rethink how the innumerable agencies of the natural world relate and come to be. So we must ask the question of *generativity*. Both Brassier and Grant, I believe, have successfully asked this question—and wrestling with possible answers is certainly a project worth extending.

Despite recognizing this picture regarding the natural world, its sources of generativity, there are however, I think, stabilizing values of equilibrium and harmony —where again, contrasts of value establish larger scale compositions that enhance rather than detract from any agencies' assertion or will to life. This is where the concepts of "civilization" and "society" come to play (and thus Whitehead but also Hegel). And if we give up the idea of "Nature" as super-order or container we must also give up the opposite view that nature is just particular objects or *discreta* to the exclusion of the ecological relationships found between and among things, where these relationships are themselves not just "things." We ought to focus on the natural world's processes, activities, and relationships at risk of focusing on items of the world as some catalog of static, frozen instants. This is all to say that we must acknowledge that larger scale compositions and networks are possible: universality is just as real as any particular, and is indeed distinct from the particular as abstract generality. This is the basis of how mathematics and logic both are, or can be, the "backbone" of any metaphysics seeking cosmological or environmental conclusions.

The adventure of the natural world and the agencies within it is far from over. There are excellent resources that many philosophers today, Brassier and Grant among them, are using in order to carry forward the conversation. It is only recently that Continental philosophy has picked up the idea of "nature" in its metaphysics, but that is the invitation that I personally would like to pick up in my own work. I think that there should be a Continental "philosophy of nature" which keeps in mind the speculative moment that I have discussed yet attempts to ground itself both in the empirical facts of nature and the rational sciences: science, cosmology, rationality, mathematics, and logic. There is no reason why we ought to stop asking such fundamental or ultimate questions now. But this is how I see my own project of speculative naturalism relating to developments in contemporary metaphysics.

With that said I hope that the readers of this book will find the philosophies presented herein as inspirational as I have found them, and, while taking these philosophers on their own terms, can use the concepts and ideas they have fashioned to then fashion one's *own* speculative philosophy that extends even further the speculative philosophical enterprise—past the boundaries which have grown around it, boundaries put there by online factions or blog kingpins who have attempted to throttle by the neck the speculative spirit that was—through a 2007 conference called "Speculative Realism"—attempting to birth new directions, new ideas, and new concepts.

Resources for Further Reading

Brassier, Ray, interviewed by Marcin Rychter, "I Am a Nihilist because I Still Believe in Truth." *Kronos* March 4, 2011: http://kronos.org.pl/numery/kronos-1-162011/kronos-1162011/.

Brassier, Ray, *Nihil Unbound: Enlightenment and Extinction* (Basingstoke: Palgrave MacMillan, 2007).

Brassier, Ray, interviewed by Richard Marshall, "Nihil Unbound: Interview with Richard Marshall." *3:AM Magazine* online: http://www.3ammagazine.com/3am/nihil-unbound/.

Brassier, Ray, "Transcendental Logic and True Representings." *Glass Bead Journal*, Site 0: "Castalia, The Game of Ends and Means," February 2016: http://www.glass-bead.org/article/transcendental-logic-and-true-representings/?lang=enview.

Brassier, Ray, "Wandering Abstraction: Acceleration, Communization, and Real Movement." *Mute Magazine*, February 13, 2014: http://www.metamute.org/editorial/articles/wandering-abstraction.

Hamilton Grant, Iain, *Philosophies of Nature after Schelling* (London and New York: Continuum, 2008).

Notes

1 Brassier, "Transcendental Logic and True Representings," http://stasisjournal.net/all-issues/12-1-politics-of-negativity-october-2013/14-that-which-is-not-philosophy-as-entwinement-of-truth-and-negativitym, henceforward abbreviated as TWiN.
2 Grant, *Philosophies of Nature after Schelling*, 6.
3 Back Door Broadcasting academic podcast, Accelerationism: questions after session 1, Mark Fisher and Ray Brassier: http://backdoorbroadcasting.net/2010/09/accelerationism/ | transcribed online at: https://moskvax.wordpress.com/2010/09/30/accelerationism-questions-after-session-1-mark-fisher-and-ray-brassier/.
4 See "Interview with Ray Brassier" by Leon Niemoczynski, *After Nature* blog.
5 Brassier, *Nihil Unbound*, 3.
6 Brassier, TWiN.
7 Brassier, TWiN.
8 Brassier, TWiN.
9 Brassier, TWiN.
10 Brassier, TWiN.
11 Brassier, TWiN.
12 Brassier, TWiN.
13 Brassier, TWiN.
14 Grant, *Philosophies of Nature after Schelling*, 1.
15 See Schelling, *First Outline of a System of the Philosophy of Nature* (New York: SUNY Press, 2004), 5, 14–15.

16 Schelling, *First Outline of a System of the Philosophy of Nature*, 16.
17 Grant, *Philosophies of Nature after Schelling*, 1.
18 Grant, *Philosophies of Nature after Schelling*, 1.
19 Grant, *Philosophies of Nature after Schelling*, 3.
20 Grant, *Philosophies of Nature after Schelling*, 5.
21 Grant, *Philosophies of Nature after Schelling*, 6.
22 Grant, *Philosophies of Nature after Schelling*, 7.
23 Grant, *Philosophies of Nature after Schelling*, 8.
24 Grant, *Philosophies of Nature after Schelling*, 9.
25 Grant, *Philosophies of Nature after Schelling*, 5.
26 Grant, *Philosophies of Nature after Schelling*, 19.
27 Grant, *Philosophies of Nature after Schelling*, xi.
28 Grant, *Philosophies of Nature after Schelling*, 27.
29 Grant, *Philosophies of Nature after Schelling*, 27.
30 Grant, *Philosophies of Nature after Schelling*, 28.
31 Grant, *Philosophies of Nature after Schelling*, 28.
32 Grant, *Philosophies of Nature after Schelling*, 33.
33 Sparrow had once revealed to me during a December meeting of the APA that this was why he chose ontology of objects. When questioned why, he responded in the manner of shallow range empiricism, "That's what I observe, objects." But he spoke nothing of any objects' *generation*.
34 Grant, *Philosophies of Nature after Schelling*, viii.

Interview with Ray Brassier
by Leon Niemoczynski (2017)

Ray Brassier is so far best known for his popular work, *Nihil Unbound: Enlightenment and Extinction* (Palgrave Macmillan, 2007; 2010), however he has since developed his philosophical project and moved beyond many of the positions he first articulated in that book. This interview first took place in 2012 but was updated in 2017 to reflect the many developments which have occurred in the course of Brassier's philosophical project.

1. Leon Niemoczynski: How did you first become interested in philosophy, and what led you to decide that you'd like to pursue a career in philosophy (whether teaching or research)? How did you end up in your current position at the American University of Beirut?

Ray Brassier: I became interested in philosophy when I was relatively young (13), but it took a long time for me to decide I wanted to pursue it academically. I did not enjoy school and had no desire to go to university, which was not an option anyway since I was a terrible student and did not have the requisite qualifications. I was 27 when I eventually managed to enroll for a philosophy degree at university. I decided to pursue it as far as I could simply because it was more important to me than anything else. But I had no career plan and am astonished I managed to get any sort of academic employment. I view my academic career as a wholly unexpected but very welcome piece of good fortune. I ended up in Beirut entirely by chance. I wanted to get out of London and was lucky enough to be offered a position at AUB.

2. LN: In a recent talk in Berlin, you mention Bergson, Deleuze, and Whitehead and how those philosophers have been recently appropriated within contemporary scholarship (I believe at one point you make reference to Iain Hamilton Grant, whose philosophy I also take a great interest in). How do you appropriate Bergson or other like-philosophers (you also mentioned Bergson in Zagreb), and how does his thought play out within your work? Is there a philosophy of life or anti-life, vitalism or anti-vitalism, a beyond or "after" vitalism, working within your perspective?

RB: I'm very critical of Bergson and of vitalism more generally. Nevertheless, I think Bergson is an important philosopher who often asks the right questions, even if I think his answers are wrong. I'm not interested in proposing a philosophy of life or anti-life, but in querying the inflation of "life" into a master-category in contemporary philosophy, not just by overt vitalists, but also by phenomenologists, critical theorists, and enactivists. I'm a great admirer of Iain and think our projects overlap in very interesting ways. I'm particularly interested in his work on "the physics of the Idea." This ties into the question of Plato's relation to naturalism, which is of enormous importance for me. The philosopher in whom this connection is developed in the most ingenious and unexpected fashion is Wilfrid Sellars, which is why he has become such an indispensable resource for my work. Sellars is a Kantian philosopher who also adumbrated a process metaphysics, which is why his thought is so uniquely challenging, both for Kantian anti-metaphysicians and anti-Kantian metaphysicians. He takes up themes from Bergson's metaphysics of duration but subjects it to a Kantian transformation that renders it compatible with empirical science.

3. LN: In your Berlin talk as well, there is a lot of ground covered with Plato. It's also known that you have an interest in philosophical naturalism. How does Plato fit into your philosophical naturalism—if at all—and what might we learn from Plato according to your project? (This seemed to be a major point of your talk.)

RB: Plato is a key touchstone for me. I think his separation of truth from *doxa*, and of the idea from the sensible, is the inaugural and indispensable gesture of all philosophizing. He's also the founder of philosophy as dialectics, which I'm interested in reaffirming, having overcome my long aversion to its caricatured forms. Basically, I'm interested in reconciling Platonism with naturalism by reconciling the dialectics of the idea with the dynamism of the sensible. This is also a way of reconciling idealism with materialism, which I think is necessary. Again, Sellars is the key inspiration here.

4. **LN:** To follow up on the question regarding your interest in Plato and how Plato may be of use within your own philosophical naturalism, I'd like to ask a question about location, particularly with respect to the perspectives of idealism and materialism as well as philosophical naturalism and transcendental philosophy. In a rather provocative quote you state,

> I consider myself an idealist, as opposed to a materialist, as I insist on the need to preserve the relative autonomy of thinking, and the cogency and the consistency of thinking, and of conceptual rationality, precisely in order to be able to adjudicate the relationship between thinking and reality, between theory and practice, and the conditions for practice [...] If you try to fuse thought into material reality indiscriminately, I think that leads to an impotent short-circuit [...] Not to put too fine a point on it, so that you can maintain and generate a locus of rational agency. In other words, keep a space of subjectivation open that provides a prism for practical incision, a point of insertion. And that has to be done, and

> I think this involves re-examining the legacy of Hegel, and of Hegelianism [...] I would insist on the need to preserve the autonomy of rationality as something that allows you to intervene, to cut, in the continuity.

There is a lot here that I think reveals some of the trajectory we have seen in some of your most recent work. But I want to start with "the need to preserve the autonomy of thinking, conceptual rationality, so as to adjudicate between thought and reality or between theory and practice," the "conditions" for practice, as you say. We spoke about Iain Grant whose dynamics of the sensible or "physics of the Idea" engages the Idea by reading Plato as a one-world theorist. This entails, he argues, that any naturephilosophy (here read in this question as naturalism) must "embed materialism within the orbit of Platonism" to rebuke any Kantian eliminativism that regards the Idea as a mere form of our understanding, a mere "categorial given." And here Grant takes the Idea to mean an "agent of nature" (cause) although acting so in a non-sensible manner.

My question is, there seems to be a tension between idealism and materialism, or between naturalism and transcendental philosophy perhaps more concretely, in the need to maintain the insertion point of which you speak, the insertion point for the autonomy of reason, conceptual rationality, a "space of subjectivation." Without bluntly calling the Idea nature or nature Idea, nor without simplistically compounding the two, the most pressing question presented in this seems to be how we might account for the locus of the Idea within a naturalistic register—and how to do so without compromising its autonomy. To treat the locus of subjectivation strictly as a psychologistic cognitive affair (ideas or conceptual systems are merely "in" the mind unrelated to external spatiotemporal coordinates or even social practices) seems to run the risk of either the nominalization of truth or its perspectivalization (or at the very least it seems to compromise the integrity of conceptuality's autonomy as much as it begs the question "where"); but on the other hand, by releasing the autonomy of conceptuality and subjectivation, rational agency, one runs the risk of an egregious transcendentalism in the name of transcendental philosophy; that is, supernaturalism in the form of Plato as two-world theorist or a kind of "myth of the given" for a priori processes of subjectivation that take on a supernatural character whose existence in-itself is to be taken on faith (one reading of Kant).

The question concerning the locus of the Idea seems legitimate if we are to maintain that nature is intelligible within a register of naturalism—which is to say, it seems we must understand how nature's intelligibility is so if one is to maintain a commitment to naturalism at all. What are your thoughts concerning the locus of subjectivation and the status of the Idea within a philosophical naturalism such as the one you endorse? Even if there are physical or material correlates for the Idea it seems its activity must be accounted for given its objectivating structure.

RB: I'll begin with idealism and the status of the Idea then move on to the issue of subjectivity. By "idealism" in the quote you cite above I mean a commitment to the irreducibility of the conceptual. Whether or not this entails embracing realism about the Idea is a difficult issue. We'd have to get clear about the distinction between the concept and the Idea, which is not an easy task. My minimal definition of a concept would be Kantian: anything that can assume a predicative role. The predicative function is linguistically instantiated and so neither mental nor physical: reifying concepts as entities is a category mistake. Concepts have functional coordinates but not spatiotemporal ones. If the Idea is understood as some sort of integrated totality of concepts, whose structure is neither psychological, nor linguistic, nor even socio-historical, then the Idea transcends specific localization as well as determinate categorization. This is not to say that it is supernatural: refusing to reify is not the same as refusing to naturalize. The Idea would be the integrated whole presupposed by any system of functionally differentiated concepts. It need not be restricted to a regulative role, as it is in Kant. I'm even willing to countenance the salience of something like Hegel's absolute Idea to make sense of the claim that concepts come in integrally differentiated unities, so long as the differentiation encompasses contradiction. The Idea as contradictory whole would transcend categorization and localization but then of course its self-moving character would swallow nature. Something dismembers the unity of the Idea beyond its own auto-generative contradictoriness. But I'm not sure I would call it "nature." I'm uneasy about any metaphysical naturalism that identifies nature with physis in the pre-modern sense of "surging-forth." Modern physics is the dismembering of ancient physis: nature is not-one. I take this to be a non-negotiable cognitive advance. To be a modern naturalist is to admit that nature is replete with intelligible discontinuities, whose recognition reminds us not just that essentializing is always premature, but that nature works through the inessential, the accidental. So it's not clear to me what it means to "situate" the Idea, whether in nature or anywhere else. Having said this, I am sympathetic to the suggestion that the Idea be understood as an "agent of nature" exercising a supersensible—which does not mean supernatural—agency. And I agree that any naturalism worthy of the name ought to explain how (if not why) nature is intelligible. I think these two commitments come together in the idea that the autonomy of the concept is indissociable from the autonomy of action. This is perfectly crystallized in Sellars' dictum: "Inferring is an act." Conceptual autonomy (which is ideal) abuts onto practical autonomy. Rationality is a condition of agency.

This is where the issue of the subject and of subjectivation comes in. Here I think Hegel achieves a decisive advance over Kant in his conception of the subject as a gap or discontinuity in the positive order of being, or substance. Kant's "thing that thinks" is not a substance, but the claim that its apperceptive function is realized by a community of knowers encourages a dualism of function and *vehicule*, or norms and causes. Transcendental synthesis, or the apperceptive function, is not a thing in the world, but its logical power must be causally realized by something in the world. Without this realization, it is nothing: an empty abstraction, a mere thought entity, or what Kant calls "an empty concept without an object." Ideal function requires a real substrate. Were the concept capable of exercising its causal power independently of any physical substrate, transcendental idealism would give way to metaphysical idealism. The insistence on a distinction that is irreducible in one dimension (concepts ≠ causes) while being reducible in another (concepts are nothing over and above causes) threatens to turn into a dualism, i.e., an unarticulated distinction. I think this is what threatens to stymie even the most sophisticated forms of naturalized Kantianism, such as Sellars' or Brandom's (if one considers that Brandom's Hegel is still very Kantian). So what articulates logical power and causal power, reasons and causes? I think Hegel saw that any attempt to bridge the gap from one side or the other leads either to dogmatic rationalism ("the ideal is the real") or skeptical empiricism ("the ideal is not real"). Instead, Hegel develops a vision where the gap between the ideal and the real is constitutive of the subject. The subject is no longer a transcendental form whose empirical anchoring defies analysis; it is the split that articulates the conceptual order and the causal order. I think subjectivation occurs through a mode of occurrence that requires an eventual conception of time (I think this is what is most profoundly Hegelian in Badiou). I think Hegel's "speculative revolution" vis-à-vis rationalism, empiricism, and (Kantian) criticism can be summarized in the five following points:

1) Speculation beyond representation: the contradictoriness of the absolute Idea allows

us to think time independently of substantial movement (change as exchange of contraries; time as the number of motion with respect to before and after).

2) Speculative knowing versus absolute representation: not "we will know everything," but "there is nothing we will not know."

3) The whole is not completed actuality (i.e., consummated potency) but occurrent incompleteness: now-time (*Jetztzeit*), understood as the time that demands to be comprehended as ours, is the split between what has been and what will be. The absolute is the occurrent actuality (*Wirklichkeit*) of substanceless time: the contemporaneity that philosophy must comprehend.

4) Represented substance is conceptless exteriority: space-time as forms of intuition. So long as substance (objectivity) is represented, conceptual necessity remains extrinsic to substantial determination.

5) Self-reflecting substance is the subject as notional (conceptual) self-relation, i.e., indivision as division (essence as contradiction). The actuality of the absolute is substance-becoming-subject as temporal rupture. Absolute knowing is the effectuation of this rupture.

From the claim that the absolute is the occurrentness of time beyond representation and intuition, a discontinuity in what is represented as being's substantial continuity, there follows a conception of subjectivity as the comprehensive effectuation of this discontinuity; in other words, the rationalization of the irrational, or formalization of formlessness. This is the conception I am interested in developing.

5. LN: In your recently published article "Transcendental Logic and True Representings" you write that, "The goal of cognitive enquiry consists in incorporating ever more facts about the structure of representing into every represented fact. This would be the naturalization of the involuted spiral of absolute knowing. In this sense, spatiotemporal location provides the transcendental coordinates for our species' collective world story. [...] As it progresses, the history of what we know incorporates within itself more and more facts about the empirical structure of knowing. The limit of this movement would be the point at which empirical (sigma-tau) facts about the structure of knowing are incarnated in the structure of empirical (spatiotemporal) facts." As I read this two things came to mind: first, obviously Hegel in your allusion to the involuted spiral of absolute knowing; but second, C.S. Peirce and other pragmatic naturalists who possess an interest in scientific discovery, truth, and the development of natural science as a process of enquiry.

In this question I'd like to ask you about another tension which often arises within naturalism, but this time between idealism and realism, particularly among the pragmatists who appeal to the accumulation of ever more facts within an incarnational story of knowing. The "spiral of knowing" of spatiotemporal facts, as well as the involuted knowing of the structure of knowing which knows fact, is in one sense unlimited regarding how one might interpret nature to be an unending complexity of spatiotemporal fact. In other words, there is a tradition which sees the cognitive enterprise as belonging to a story of knowing that ceaselessly and continually calibrates and re-calibrates itself to the structural infinitude of nature of which knowing and the structure of knowing is part. (And by structural infinitude what I mean to point to is the limitless diversity present in potential internal to nature itself; thus affording through evolutionary processes the ever-present opportunity to "surprise" mind with new fact.)

My question is, do you believe the empirical structure of knowing is unlimited in the same way given that, as we might suppose (and according to Sellars, whom you cite at the beginning of your article) the "mind that gains knowledge of the world of which it is a part" involves "in its acquisition of knowledge [...] [its] being acted on or 'affected' by the objects it knows"? Is cognitive enquiry in the long run necessarily a bounded venture given the potentially limitless evolution and activity of the objects we seek to know, coupled with the structural, nomic, and descriptive complexity found within the empirical structure of knowing itself? Perhaps more clearly, how are we to gauge the adequacy of our explanations, the veracity of our knowledge, the truth of our reasons given the prospect that the structure of knowing in this continuing story of knowledge may know no end? How does one gain epistemological traction in the story of incarnational knowing? Is there broader implication for an imperfectibility of knowing? To close, I am wondering how this might relate to your thoughts about the process of cognitive enquiry with respect to science and the Enlightenment, the goals and aims of not only cognitive enquiry generally but science particularly, and whether you believe that some form of postulated normative ends might be necessary (as in Nicholas Rescher or C.S. Peirce, or Kant for example, the regulative ideal for the end of all enquiry; the regulative rationale for supposing a cognitive inexhaustibility of nature so enquiry could be said to move "forward").

RB: I would say the process of cognitive enquiry is unbounded in the long run. Although it incorporates radical epistemic shifts, my wager is that it is still possible to identify underlying continuities across these shifts; were this not so we would have to give up on the very idea of knowing as a continuous collective undertaking. My interest in Sellars' work is due in no small part to his account of cognitive enquiry as a "self-correcting enterprise." Cognitive evolution is a self-conscious process motivated by reasons, and not simply a mechanism determined by causes. This is to say by our self-consciousness about the scope and function of our concepts. The claim that there is no unitary thing called "knowing" is of course the basic claim of cultural relativism, which is particularly prevalent in the humanities nowadays. I reject it: however varied and multifaceted its manifestations, there is such a think as knowledge and it is the common resource of homo sapiens.

6. LN: Your insistence on rationality and its central importance within the speculative enterprise has drawn criticism from certain quarters (whom you address quite brilliantly, in my opinion) in the Postscript to Peter Wolfendale's book published by Urbanomic in 2014. The charge is that any such insistence upon reason and rationality results in a "mindless rationalism" that propagates a "neurology deathcult" "brainwashing" those convinced (by argument, mind you) into becoming "rationalist mind-slaves." As Wolfendale summarizes the criticism, its language also takes on the various permutations in charging those who insist upon such a central role for reason and rationality as being "'scientism', 'nihilism', 'eliminativism', 'pessimism', in combination with sundry negative adjectives and faux-renegade imagery. [Your] modus operandi is to destroy all that is wholesome and good in Continental philosophy, through a combination of perfidious science worship and mellifluous brainwashing of impressionable grad students." The honor of being the target of this criticism has been shared by Pete Wolfendale himself, Terence Blake (a French philosopher of science and pluralism, speculative empiricism, and who is known for his work on the philosophy of Laruelle), and bizarrely, myself (considering my own insistence upon rationality as being required to indiscriminately engage in metaphysics-as-speculation, given rationality's ability to free thought from constraints of immanence although not from all constraints; and in my case this charge is especially interesting considering my own axiological commitments which conceive of the natural world's ontological integrity in quasi-pietist terms: the natural world is always capable of "overturning" even our most steadfast of beliefs, where humility before the natural world seems required, even within the sciences). Nevertheless, is an insistence upon rationality as dangerous as we are told that it is? On a related point, I should mention that my own thought has been that, if anything, it is only through the rational deployment of concepts that reason can indeed be utilized in its extrahumam capacity capable of extending beyond the human although encompassing of it, and this does nothing but aid metaphysical endeavor—and so one has not a powerful (merely) psychologistic tool but indeed a realist, metaphysical one. (It is for this reason that it seems to be that rationality, reason, is more inhuman than human.) On my view, it is the sheer power and scope of reason taken as speculative instrument—yet granting its autonomy as an instrument—that rationality can deliver a more adequate ontology capable of incorporating features of reality within a robustly naturalistic register, features beyond those limited to human experience so-called or the phenomenality of appearances to human consciousness (e.g., phenomenology). Again, rationality is part of nature and it is nature which we seek to know. The power, scope, and uniformity afforded the employment of rationality within one's own ontology (under-girding any epistemology) seems therefore only to be a contribution to the stability and integrity of one's metaphysics, not a danger. But perhaps I am incorrect. I wonder what your thoughts on the matter happen to be. What is the role of rationality in your project and is stress upon rationality within metaphysics somehow "dangerous?" Tongue in cheek perhaps, but is any philosophical emphasis on rationality a contribution to the destruction of "all that is wholesome and good in Continental philosophy?"

RB: If one were looking for a term guaranteed to draw the ire of Continental philosophers across the board, it would not be "realism" or "materialism" but "reason." The reduction of reasoning to "calculation," "instrumental rationality," "logocentrism," "identity thinking," etc., is the common thread running through almost all 20th-century Continental philosophy. But my interest in defending rationality is not merely contrarian. Initially, it was sparked by my incredulity at the absurd caricatures of rationality promulgated within the Continental tradition, together with my growing awareness of a direct link between the demotion of rationality and the embrace of the ineffable, the incomprehensible, the wholly other, etc. I am not much moved by the pathos of the ineffable, although I find sophisticated expressions of mysticism philosophically instructive. But one needs to have understood a lot to be entitled to proclaim the limits of understanding and sadly this is not the case with most partisans of the ineffable. My conviction is that only reason is entitled to fix the limits of reason: this was Plato's conviction, as it was Kant's and Hegel's. Anyone wishing to contest reason's right to carry out its own critique needs to justify their appeal to an authority higher than reason and this is precisely what cannot be done since reason is justification: absolute exemption from rational justification can never be rationally justified (though of course certain claims or beliefs may be relatively exempt, depending on the context). The proper response to the claim that something transcends justification is simply to ask: says who? Whatever transcends justification has had that transcendent status bestowed upon it by someone: nothing has absolute authority in and of itself; this is the simple corollary of atheism; indeed, theism just is endowing some phenomenon or instance with absolute authority. The ruin of theism is prefigured by Socrates' question to Euthyphro: "Is it right because God commands it, or does God command it because it is right?" This is why those who claim that the premium on rationality is continuous with theism are mistaken. They are confusing rationalism as a metaphysical hypothesis, the claim that everything exists for a reason, which is indeed theistic, with rationality as a semantic constraint, the claim that you cannot mean or believe what you cannot give a reason for. Rationality in this semantic sense was espoused by Plato, Kant, and Hegel, even if it was not entirely disentangled from its metaphysical sense. It is the motor of atheism because it insists that to think something or to say something is to give and ask for reasons for it: anyone who cannot or will not do so is not actually thinking or saying anything.

What separates rationality as a semantic constraint from rationalism as a metaphysical postulate is the question of implementation, the focus on reasoning as an activity, rather than a supernatural faculty. With the shift from reason as supernatural faculty to reasoning as material practice, rationality is demystified. Turing's mathematization of thinking—the equation of thinking with computation—contributes decisively to this demystification. It paves the way for a functionalist conception of thinking whose crux is the claim that semantic differences can be syntactically encapsulated. The question then is whether theoretical reasoning has explanatory priority over practical reasoning or vice versa. This is also the question of the relation between formal and material inference. Sellars makes a decisive contribution here because he overturns the subordination of semantic content to logical form and suggests that the former is rooted in the latter: material inference is the condition for formal inference, which allows one to say what one is doing when one engages in material inference. The primacy of material inference leads to a conception of language where semantic rules provide the framework within which logical rules serve to make explicit what speakers are doing when they make assertions. Logic becomes, in Brandom's words, "the organ of semantic self-consciousness." It plays a regulative role in our discursive activity by allowing us to say what we are doing when we say something. In other words, the development of logic allows us to reason about reason. The crucial point is that this reflexive reasoning, or self-conscious rationality, emerges out of everyday discursive practice. Overturning the subordination of semantic content to logical form allows us to understand reasoning as an activity in which we are "always already" engaged as soon as we think or say anything. Every challenge to rationality presupposes the resources of rationality: some of these challenges may help revise and refine those resources, but none will ever defeat them.

Moreover, rationality in this semantic sense is the defining feature of homo sapiens only to the extent that homo sapiens instantiate it. Rationality is definitive of humanity; humanity is not definitive of rationality. There is nothing necessarily human about rationality: non-human intelligences or reasoners are perfectly envisageable. Developing a theory of general artificial intelligence is one of the most exciting prospects opened up by rationalism. In this regard, inferentialism offers instructive correctives to standard computationalism by insisting that inference requires a grasp of content. However, insofar as it maintains the distinction between content and *vehicule*, inferentialism perpetuates Kant's dualism of function and cause. The really interesting question is whether the inferentialist account of reasoning suffices to account for the most sophisticated varieties of philosophical rationality, as exemplified by Hegel's own "speculative thinking," which is notorious for proposing to exempt reason from the law of non-contradiction. Inferentialism overthrows the subordination of semantic content to logical form but it maintains the subordination of content to non-contradiction by insisting that contents are determined by incompatibility relations. This is a profound issue which I can't hope to address properly here save to say I don't think the crucial role Hegel allots to contradiction can be accounted for in terms of incompatibility. More importantly still, the controversy over Hegel's rationalism is whether contradictions are real or merely ideal. I think the question may be badly posed insofar as Hegel's point is that the juxtaposition presupposes an underlying continuity, but one that cannot be substantialized. Real and ideal are poles of a continuum whose fabric cannot be consistently grasped in terms of either. Contradiction is the marker of intelligible discontinuity, and as such it is a counter to metaphysical rationalism and a resource for naturalism.

7. LN: Given your recent success with the much-acclaimed *Nihil Unbound*, what are your reflections on that book now, especially as that book may relate to your research that will be appearing in the future? You've mentioned that you are working on a number of things right now, what areas of research (or theses) should we expect to see? Another book perhaps? What should we expect from you in the future—in terms of articles, another book, or upcoming talks? Please feel free to share any last words and end as you'd like.

RB: I regard the book as a botched job. It contends that nature is not the repository of purpose and that consciousness is not the fulcrum of thought. The cogency of these claims presupposes an account of thought and meaning that is neither Aristotelian—everything has meaning because everything exists for a reason—nor phenomenological—consciousness is the basis of thought and the ultimate source of meaning. The absence of any such account is the book's principal weakness (it has many others, but this is perhaps the most serious). It wasn't until after its completion that I realized Sellars' account of thought and meaning offered precisely what I needed. To think is to connect and disconnect concepts according to proprieties of inference. Meanings are rule-governed functions supervening on the pattern-conforming behavior of language-using animals. This distinction between semantic rules and physical regularities is dialectical, not metaphysical. To evoke it is to commit oneself to a qualified version of anthropocentrism, which I'm quite prepared to defend. It's of a piece with the distinction between sapience and sentience, which is fundamental for Sellars. I've been working my way through his writings since completing *Nihil Unbound* and my understanding of his thought has progressed considerably since my brief (and woefully inadequate) treatment of it there. His influence will feature prominently in the book I'm currently working on, tentatively entitled *That Which Is Not*. It will be about the reality of appearance, a topic which was not properly addressed in *Nihil Unbound*. The challenge of rationalism is to insist on the distinction between appearance and reality, or the sensible and the intelligible, while accounting for the reality of appearances, or the intelligibility of the sensible. This is a problem that goes back to Plato. It's a question of understanding how every appearance has a kind of reality, but only insofar as it is split from within by what it does not reveal. This ties into the issues of the intelligibility of becoming and the structure of time. These are themes that were touched upon but not properly worked through in *Nihil Unbound*. My other long-term project is a book about historical materialism and revisionary naturalism. But it's premature to talk about it right now since it's still at a very early stage.

8. LN: Thanks so much for taking time to do this interview, Ray. It's been a pleasure and I am even more curious now where your future work may be headed. If you would ever like to inform philosophical readers online of what you're up to (especially talks—I missed your talk at Cornell because I just didn't hear about it online until it actually appeared on Cornell's website) then please feel free to email me and I can make an announcement informally on my website. In any case, hopefully we'll have the pleasure of meeting one day in person. Best of luck to you and thanks again.

RB: Very good. Thanks for your kind offer, I'll certainly bear it in mind.

Interview with Iain Hamilton Grant
by Leon Niemoczynski (2013)

This interview was originally published in *Cosmos and History* Vol. 9, No. 2 (2013): 32–43.

1. Leon Niemoczynski: Tell us, how did you get started in philosophy? What made you become a philosopher?

Iain Hamilton Grant: Two things got me started: art and material. Before I discovered that limitations of talent and technique made this improbable, I was attempting to be a performance artist, a sculptor, and a musician and had therefore enrolled on a BA Fine Art at Reading University. During this time, I was working on a series of figures, in various media (copperplate, charcoal, silk-screen, and acrylics), derived from headlamp-glare on the rain-soaked windscreen that absorbed my attention on a ten-hour night-time bus journey from London to Edinburgh. The figure formed by light and rain on a moving screen reconstructed these physical elements as if constructing a four-dimensional account of the dynamics of Kandinsky's and Malevich's most abstract compositions. This was the first move toward philosophy: abstraction and actuality are identical. The second had more to do with the material, and stemmed from working in metal. The physical hardness of metal is an alterable state, so that in welding, it becomes liquid or can be drawn through with an electrical arc with less resistance than paper exerts on charcoal, was my Platonic moment, such that matter, the "darkest of all things," revealed its capacity to become at the expense of its apparent solidity, its secure three-dimensional massiveness. Art taught me the fluidity of cave-bound appearance and that it could be pierced, that something lay on the other side of appearance that possessed a reality all the more striking for being impalpable, yet palpably achieved. At the same time, what were to me the exceedingly strange thoughts and forms communicated by the abstract languages developed in Joyce, Cage, and Heidegger (whose *Being and Time* I had begun to appreciate, albeit less for its meaning than its extraordinary means), were becoming more immediate means to realize the aims my more or less "artistic" investigations of matter had initiated. I began therefore to attend first-year Philosophy classes, which began to introduce discipline into my thoughts, and that was it: the concept cut through more reality more quickly than the arc-welder through sheet-steel, and did so more impressively. If art had been for me the technique whereby the manipulability of reality was first demonstrated, philosophy now became a continuation of art by different means. I was fortunate while in Reading to be able to pursue my peculiar and unschooled fascination with Heidegger and, while following the traditional Anglo-American curriculum of logic, semantics, and philosophy of science, to have enjoyed classes on Kant, Hegel, and even Whitehead.

2. LN: You are the author of *Philosophies of Nature after Schelling* (2006) and as a co-author, *Idealism: The History of a Philosophy* (2011). A theme which seems to undergird both of these books is that contemporary philosophy has yet to grasp the full creative potential of the Idea as it is registered in philosophical idealism, and that there are possibilities in contemporary philosophy for idealism where idealism can be understood in such a way that it need not necessarily exclude important dynamics found within naturalism, materialism, and realism. I am wondering if you can speak specifically to the relationship between naturalism—or better yet, a "philosophy of nature" as you articulate it within your books—and the task of what you refer to as the "non-eliminative Idealism" proposed by Schelling, whom you closely follow but also modify. Specifically, elements of such a philosophy also appear in Bergson, Whitehead, or Peirce, but it is Schelling's naturephilosophy that is most important for you (it is probably important to note here just how close philosophically Peirce and Schelling were to each other, especially with respect to their outlooks concerning philosophical cosmology and physics). But it is Plato's "physics of the Idea" that you knit with Schellingean naturephilosophy instead, which in its own right yields some very unique insights and which has been an interest of yours for quite some time. What are some of the more important and fruitful connections between Schellingean idealism, Platonic philosophy, and philosophical naturalism, as you see it? How might these connections prove useful for 21st-century speculative philosophy? I am curious to know whether your research into Schelling and Plato at any point has crossed paths with Peirce's own philosophy of nature, given the influences and connections involved?

IHG: Before discussing Peirce, philosophical cosmology, and the philosophy of nature, I would like to outline some general conceptions concerning the Idea and the character of Idealist philosophy to which the earlier part of your question alludes.

As directly as possible, idealism is that philosophy that affirms the reality of the Idea. The point is not that any account of reality must be from the standpoint of the Idea, of the Ideal, or that the conceptual is insuperable, as for example McDowell has it; but rather that reality is incompletely furnished unless the Idea is included in it. Idealism is therefore eliminative just when the Idea is accounted the species of which other entities—usually nature or matter, but also appearances—are genera. Nothing in this case is or can be on the far side of the concept. This is eliminative in that it doesn't allow that the Idea be the Idea while nature be nature; rather the one must become an instance of the other, and the problem is exactly the same whether posed from the perspective of eliminative idealism or eliminative materialism.

Idealism, when not eliminative, it seems to me—and I am particularly fond of pointing to some of its less read exemplars, such as Bosanquet or Pringle-Pattison—does not seek to account for one thing in terms of another, but for each thing exactly as it is. Such a view is evident in the fact that, for example, Plato's *auto kath'auto* has less to do with Kant's *Ding an sich* than with a simpler "itself by itself": it is a causal account of subjectivity independent of consciousness, or the "it-attractor" by which whatever becomes becomes what it is.

To make the point as clear as possible, imagine an intrascientific contest regarding the actuality of the Idea. On the one hand, neuroscientists successfully eliminate talk of ideation from talk of brain structures, wherein nothing resembling "the Idea" is discovered. On the other, physics discovers that the Idea is an actuality. What is proven? That the Idea is not amongst the furniture of mentality but amongst that of actuality. This, it strikes me, is the Platonic tradition, and it is something that Schelling recovers—note the extended, critical discussion of the "substantiality" or "physical existence of the Idea" in the *Timaeusschrift* (70–73, 30–37), for example, or the following passage from the 1804 *System of Philosophy as a Whole*:

> Merely reflective humanity has no idea of an objective reason, of an Idea that as such is utterly real and objective; all reason is something subjective to them, as equally is everything ideal, and the idea itself has for them only the meaning of a subjectivity, so

that they therefore know only two worlds, the one consisting of stone and rubble, the other of intuitions and the thinking thereupon. (SW VI: 279)

In another direction entirely, if nature is considered the condition under which alone anything that can exist does so, then the nature that is includes precisely the Idea. Accordingly, to account for nature apart from the Idea simply misconstrues nature. But the risk of this misconstrual depends entirely on the species of our naturalism. If naturalism is based on what our best science tells us concerning nature, while this must be true if science is veridical (which if it were not would entail some very strange consequences), then the concept of nature formed on this basis depends entirely on which research programs are progressive in Lakatos' sense, and thus on what projects are being pursued. Yet no individual science has nature itself as its subject, and nor, due to ongoing questions of reducibility (for example, of biochemistry to physics), do any combination of the sciences, regardless of the period of science we are discussing, past or future. Inevitably therefore, a concept of nature formed on the basis of the best science, will be a partial concept, or a concept of part of nature. This is why a philosophy of nature is required, for if it is true that nature is that condition under which alone anything that can exist does so, then all that exists requires contextualization within a concept of nature that, by definition, cannot be exclusive or eliminative.

Further, nor can a philosophy of nature eliminate the false as such, since the generation of error is a function of at least the system of nature that produces ideation, so the capacity for error, the power of the false, must either be a part of nature or any ideation whatsoever is, merely by virtue of being such an event, true by definition. The only way a system of reason can be capable of falsity is if causal determination of the Idea is less important than its dependency: to be dependent upon nature for its production is not reducible to its being the effect of a cause, since if it is true that anything that can be is by nature alone, both the true and the false statement depend on "the nature that produces" (*e tou poiountos physis*, Plato, *Philebus*, 28a) but do so differently regardless of the causal identity of the production of ideation (i.e., that the same neurological means are employed in the production of both). Of course, taking a fully Platonic line, we may say that the Idea is precisely not produced, but rather that it is that in virtue of which there is production at all. In this case, we must introduce an additional species of causality, and not one, I think, that can easily be reduced to a species of final causation; the Idea is rather the perturbations of the finite in the infinite, as the *Philebus* says, such that the "becoming of being [*genesis eis ousian*]" is the becoming that being undergoes precisely because becoming is dependent on an end it cannot, by definition, attain. From this we gain a philosophy of nature that is neither "pulled" by ends nor "pushed" by beginnings, but one in which the dependency of whatever is on whatever else is establishes the form not only of particular existents, but also of becoming itself. The corollary of ontogenesis or the becoming of being must be the being of becoming, its form given that becoming is, or consequent upon creation having occurred in whatever manner is has, did, or will.

What I find congenial in Peirce is that neither epistemically nor cosmologically does his concept of being yield to a species of finality whose character may be determined without approximation. And it seems to me that this is a characteristic that the majority of modern philosophers of nature share: the forms of becoming may be studied in domain-specific ways, for example, by morphogenesis in the life sciences; but the forms that qua becoming, becomings must assume if becoming is what they do, impose a particular discipline upon the thinking of process that, if the world is not eternal, as Proclus thought, is not only true of, but rather part of, the becoming they articulate. Again, then, the Idea is inseparable from the actuality. This is a world of irreducible operations on which mere items in it can only consequently be isolated by an operation that achieves this. These, then, are the operations characteristic of a philosophy of nature: genesis recapitulated in the genesis of isolation cannot be reversed, such that genesis itself is isolated, without an additional operation or continuation of genesis on which that isolation depends. And here, I think, we gain insight into the complex location of the Idea in nature: it is precisely the additional dimension articulated by the operation capable of abstracting its objects from the context on which they are dependent. And so too we gain an account of the isolation function on which the particularity of inquiries into nature as such depend.

I have not made any extended study of Peirce, but what seems to me important is that philosophers of nature such as Peirce and Whitehead be recovered not merely as historical instances but rather in the context of how their inquiries into nature present the conceptualization consequent upon it as modifications of precisely that process into which they are inquiring. I am particularly interested in the development of the dialectic of the physical whereby reflection upon it augments it in the dimension of the Idea without making the Idea into the finally determining instance of a nature directed towards it. Nature thought as ontogenesis cannot but have as a consequence that the thought that nature is ontogenetic must be consequent upon an ontogenetic nature. If it does not have this consequence, it is not a thought of nature as ontogenetic.

3. LN: I want to stay with another historical question just for the moment, but this time refer to your newer co-authored book, *Idealism: The History of a Philosophy* in order to work out what philosophical idealism can offer. It is intimated that among contemporary philosophers, the full impact of Hegelian philosophy is still not fully understood. As Hegel's own philosophy of nature is "ominous" (for lack of a better way to put it), where does Hegel stand (if having any relevance for you) in your current work? I ask because you had quite a bit to say about Hegel in your talk which preceded Slavoj Zizek's talk, from this past summer of 2012. What should philosophers these days be doing with Hegel?

IHG: To ignore Hegel proves, I would agree with Foucault, to be impossible. Hence his recovery in contemporary philosophy, however attenuated such a recovery might seem on occasion to be by the mere sociality of reason rather than, as I might say, its naturalization. I will try to explain what I mean. The Hegelian problem that most interests me is how it is that for him, the *Science of Logic* completes the *Philosophy of Nature*. The latter is compromised in that its purpose is to demonstrate what we might call the consequent character of naturalistic realism, which is the function of his characterization of nature as the "self-estranged idea." It is the philosophy of nature that mediates logic and mind, the "grasp of things in thought" (*Encyclopaedia Logic* §24), insofar as to think nature entails that thing and thought be thought as mutually repulsive, and their common locus in logic shattered and suppressed, in the inevitably vain attempt to think the thing as without its thought. This is a problem not just for Hegel, but for all concept-antecedent engagements with the historicity of existence, for which the problem of nature may be taken here as shorthand. That is to say, while the rediscovery of the concept from which it turns out its object has been articulated makes the concept insuperable, the concept is a member of the historicity of existence as much as its object. The latter is indeed, in this case, consequent upon the concept, but the concept's priority in this regard is only consequently a conceptual, but antecedently a natural-historical achievement. This is why the locus of an engagement with Hegel's *Naturphilosophie* should not be the phenomenon of life, as Beiser (2008) for example argues, but rather geology, with which he briefly deals in the *Philosophy of Nature* in order to dismiss mere chronology as "of no interest to philosophy" (§24); not the orbits of the planets, but cosmogony. Granting, with Hegel, that antecedence is not a problem of chronology, neither is it reducibly a matter of conceptual interiority, which was one of Schelling's major criticisms of Hegel's logic, that in it, "the concept was everything and left nothing outside itself" (*History of Modern Philosophy*, trans. Bowie, 134). Accordingly, the historicity of the concept, for Hegel, is a matter internal to the concept, from which the historicity of things thought becomes in consequence indissociable. Yet Hegel's demand for philosophy is that its beginning be not merely the beginning of philosophy, but of everything (*Science of Logic*, trans. Millar, 67). In this contrast lies everything interesting, and Schelling's advantage. When, at the start of the Stuttgart Seminars, he poses the interrelated problems of system and philosophical beginnings, he enmeshes the beginning of philosophy in the problem of a beginning that is not its own: "To what extent is a system ever possible? I would answer that long before man decided to create a system, there already existed one, that of the world-system or cosmos" (trans. Pfau, 197). In other words, it is not thing but creation that the concept, insofar as it fails to embrace it in thought if it is thought as creation, nevertheless recapitulates creation insofar as it is thought.

Yet what Hegel presents is therefore a morphogenesis of the concept, as Bosanquet intimated in the subtitle of his own *Logic* (1911). Hegel does indeed discover rather than simply invent the movements of the concept, its functionality and its kinematics, its physics, a dimension that tends to be at once emphasized as the nature, ethos or character of the concept, and subjugated by the co-articulation of thought and thing that is the task, says Hegel, of logic insofar as it is to make a science of metaphysics. Taking this view of Hegel, and investigating the development of the functions and motions attaching to the concept, yields interesting results, insofar as the near Malevich-like "theory of the additional element" by which, in the *Differenzschrift*, on which I have been teaching a Masters course for some years now, Hegel begins to delineate his new science, would be simply a mechanical addition were it not for his discovery of the immanence of his additions to, for instance, the Kantian account of the antinomy. His procedure there already consists in discovering the movement halted by the understanding that remains therefore frustrated in reason, and thus freeing the motions of reason such that they complete the movement by retaining and augmenting their logical coordinates, so to speak, in the antinomy. Thus the additional element turns out to be the element in which the concept moves.

Logical functionalism has, of course, a post-Hegelian philosophical history in Frege and, as Ray Brassier has been excitingly showing, in Sellars' metaphysics. But it is the coordination of this with the problem Schelling embraces but Hegel elides, of creation, that yields one of the chief untapped experiments of German Idealist philosophy in general, and it is precisely ignored by any philosophical reappropriation of Hegelianism as jettisoning the problem of nature or as emphasizing only the intersubjective constitution of reason. The naturalization of logic is not simply a converse of Hegel's logicization of nature, but opens the concept, its insuperability notwithstanding, to the thought that its creation is not itself in thought. In consequence, the concept is constitutively mute with regard to that upon which it is consequent, which is ontology's recompense for Kant's demonstration that being cannot issue from reasoning. For me, these aspects of Hegel refocus attention on a problem that Platonic physics first articulated: why, if becoming is ceaseless, does it not have an *eidos* but rather power—why, that is, are power and intelligible causation non-identical? In *Philosophies of Nature after Schelling*, I argued, I now think wrongly, that the powers of the Sophist's ontology are coincident with the causality of the Idea outlined in the *Phaedo*. On the contrary, while the Idea is the grasping of the rational ground of intellection in acts of intelligence, so too production is productive even in intellection. Hence the asymmetry of the intelligible and the generative applies both to the intelligible and to the generative, and the two are indissociable.

4. **LN:** Recently some interesting overlaps between your work and Ray Brassier's have become apparent (for example, some of the ideas that have come up in each of your Berlin talks). In particular, while Brassier rejects vitalism and panpsychism outright, and while your work has come to stringently critique "traditional" vitalism and instead opt for a pluralist "neo-vitalism" of sorts (for example in the Q&A session of your Berlin talk you mention that you are not convinced that all of

panpsychism is strictly false), you also seem to have some nuanced thoughts about panpsychism—a perspective which is often related to traditional forms of vitalism. Despite your critique you choose to focus on processes of vital compulsion fueled by a transcendental ground that either in full or in part operates by a non-conceptual form of negativity, an eternal "No," where this negativity is also curiously inscribed within the dynamics of the rational as much as it is inscribed within the irrational (a very good commentary on this idea, I think, is Krell's *The Tragic Absolute* and more recently, McGrath's *Dark Ground of Spirit*). In fact, on several occasions Brassier has suggested that we return to Hegel in order to revisit, and then modify, some of these dimensions, especially regarding a sort of non-cognitive "efficacy of primary transcendental synthesis," a "self-synthesizing potency" responsible for "intensive materiality."

For both you and Brassier, then, this negativity is indeed vital in its potency, a "vital negativity" therefore. I thought that this was an interesting point of cross-over between two very differently appearing philosophies, and it is in particular how I am able to dialogue with Brassier's form of naturalism given my own interest in contemporary "neo-vitalism" (with its corresponding dynamics of the divine *Potenzen*). It seems that this all begs the question of understanding the generic scope of systematic and speculative metaphysics: how this vital negativity is involved with your concept of "ground" generally as the non-preceding yet generative condition for what is in the particular, a cosmic animating source or power that is both "creative" as much as it is destructive, but which is also "upheld" by the physics of the particular bodies it helps to animate by sharing in a mutual form of force of creation/creativity (thus "powers").

Now, you have mentioned that an upcoming book of yours may be titled *Grounds and Powers*, and that you are working on considering grounds understood as powers in the plural. Given this interesting take on negativity or ground by both you and Brassier—if I am grasping this correctly—and given that you have stated "Being unconditioned, no experience thereof is possible" (experience of this unconditioned ground is impossible), you have also stated that, "the pursuit of grounds, the descendent dimension, is a vital element of philosophy." The result of this descent is a split between thinking the unconditioned (the Absolute) as a "production monism" or experiencing it as a "production pluralism." My question is this: I am wondering with the most generic naturephilosophy in mind, despite the localization of generative powers in the plural, could we not say that the more crucial and systematically useful (or speculatively daring) question might be to consider the generic quality of the vital negative, as such? Why a many for you here rather than the one? You have meditated on this particular problematic within transcendental philosophy in your article, "The Movements of the World: The Sources of Transcendental Philosophy," and I'd like to press you on the idea of how you defend your neo-vital pluralism. That rather than considering the conditions around the orbits of things, how would you respond to the claim that we may wish to consider descendence into generative conditions as such (if we are to attain the most encompassing explanation), from processes and powers to process and power as general category (this may be a question of orientation from the particular to the general or vice versa, still, the very nature of speculative philosophy and its definition remains up for grabs—a science of the particular or an account of the whole, or some synthesis of the two).

Some philosophers have tried the conjectural and systematic route while balancing the created particulars with the source of their creation, aiming for comprehensiveness (Whitehead with his theory of creativity as a radical form of ground, but also Hartshorne and other process philosophers among whose ranks I would actually add the French philosopher Quentin Meillassoux, whose Surchaos could be understood as a fundamentally productive ground in a "process" sense). It was Meillassoux who said, "What is strange in my philosophy is that it's an ontology that never speaks about *what is* but only about what *can be*. Never about what there is because this I have no right to speak about." It seems that the conditions of generativity may possess a distinct integrity, "ultimacy" for some, that while no more "real" than what is produced, certainly deserves to be called out as an essential (perhaps even necessary) condition of creation and creativity, of contingency, and the like. What are your thoughts here concerning the varieties of transcendental philosophy in question, especially with respect to the concepts of ground, of creativity, and of their ultimacy?

IHG: Panpsychism is tempting from the point of view of an augmented naturalism. If, that is, thought is a worldly item, consistent naturalism must explain it as thought, with neurophysiology as its insufficient but necessary ground, if thought is additionally efficacious than its own actualization pathways. Because the alternative is that mindedness remains alien rather than worldly, panpsychism rejects emergence as proposing that mindedness must arise from what is without it. But temptation aside, the cost is too high: if once true, panpsychism is always true, such that mind is without beginning or end. As with the advent of life, with that of mind, the universe is irreversibly altered in its image. Not only must this again prove autochthonous, it must also propose a homogeneity-of-nature account insofar as it seeks to deny that, as Thomas Nagel puts it in *Mind and Cosmos*, the "mind-body problem is a local problem." Yet it is precisely not a local problem insofar as emergence, if true, entails that every advent is such consequently upon an antecedent with which it is neither identical nor to which it can be reduced. Thus, I can accept the panpsychist thesis that mindedness is no special case only on emergentist grounds: it is because emergence is the emergence of aliens that mindedness is not a special case.

It is because I reject the mono-causal vision of the vitalist and the homogeneity-of-nature to which panpsychism by default adheres that I am a pluralist concerning the number and nature of efficacies or powers. I see no good reason to assume that we might restrict the plausible number of causes in nature to four, two, or one, not least because the laws of the early universe might not resemble those of the later. And if this were so, in what would their "transition set," so to speak, causally consist? Precisely because they are later, I would add they cannot so resemble save in one crucial respect: every emergent is such just when it is dependent upon what it is not. And the same must apply to ground: if ground is antecedent in respect of its consequent, it is transcendentally a second-order consequent but descendentally, so to speak, a first-order issuant of that from which ground itself issues. Here there lies a philosophical decision: opt for essential reciprocity between ground and consequent, and metabolize the principle of sufficient reason; or eschew the ultimacy of grounds. Here there is a parallel with the dispositionalists in contemporary philosophy: either powers are capacities of entities, which are thus primitive with respect to powers, or entities must be consequent upon ungrounded powers. On this, Mumford's highly Schellingean "ungrounded argument" is persuasive. It is for this reason that I would draw attention to the two species of negation to which you have in turn drawn my attention via Ray's engagement with Hegel. Determinate negation (X not being not-X) is not identical to the negation of determinacy as such.

When therefore you quote me as saying that "the pursuit of grounds, the descendent dimension, is a vital element of philosophy," I do not confuse the pursuit with the possession of grounds. That this element is "vital" does not mean that it is an instance of life, but that descendence is required because no ground is ultimate. There is a dynamic tension between grounds and unground, just as between antecedent and consequent, and the conceiving of this never seals the process. The negativity of what there is not, therefore, is precisely the unconditioning of grounds consequent upon the efficacy of consequents and the unconditioned efficacy by which creation occurs, if it does.

Regarding transcendental philosophy, what I was doing in the "Movements of the World" essay was, in a word, to dispel the myth of the "single and sudden revolution" in the interests of the transcendental project. We can describe this as Kant does: the knowing that, in cognition, the objects of that cognition derive from the production of concepts, not from the causal paths of objects through the eye into the brain, as Aristotle had it. Kant's peculiar invention consists therefore not only in the negative demonstration that there are no paths from things to thoughts (the Copernican revolution), nor from thoughts to things (the elimination of existence proofs), but also in the positive demonstration that in knowing, the concept is recursive on concepts. There are, literally, powers of the concept in the mathematical sense, by means of which from conceiving anything whatever can be "deduced" a second-order knowing of the conceiving at issue. Such knowing is therefore above the "transcendental substrate" (the totality of possible predicates) in precisely the sense that only some are actualized in the knowing. It is this operativity that gives thought back its place amongst nature. Hence the pursuit of grounds, the "descendental" dimension issues precisely from the doubling of the concept. Kant's having noted that "dependency" trumps "empirical origin" (CPR A56/B80) provides a start; but because empirical origin is not the same thing as creation that the doubled concept has an indissociable externality, an "extainment set," as it were, that cannot be "resolved into reason but remains ever in the depths," as Schelling perfectly expresses it. Naturephilosophy thus entails both the extainment sets of the powers of the concept and confronts the ungrounding of nature in creation.

Thus it is creation rather than creativity with which I think speculative philosophy must be concerned if it is to sacrifice neither the powers of the concept nor the nature of which they form part. Creativity consists in the efficacy of additional powers, creation in the emergence of power where there was none. This is why the concept "thing" is, as again Schelling says, simply "the abstract concept of worldly essences" (VII, 349), and also why a powers ontology must entail their ungrounding. The only systematicity there can be is consequent upon Urchaos, as the solar system shows.

5. LN: Iain, thanks so much for taking the time to answer these questions. If you have any closing thoughts or would like to inform readers of upcoming projects, talks, or appearances, please feel free to use this space as you see fit. Please also feel free to tell us more about your forthcoming book, I am sure many are excited to hear any details that you can offer about it. Thanks so much again.

IHG: Thanks for your interest, and your complex and fascinating questions. They have made me think.

It is the above project that forms the core of my repeatedly touted but yet to be completed *Grounds and*

Powers. I will be treating of some of it, with Jason Wirth, at the Duquesne summer school on *Naturphilosophie*, which I am very much looking forward to. I also have some translations I want to publish, and some papers still in the pipeline, all of which contribute to this project. In part these will serve to make good my claim that Schelling's is a *Naturphilosophie* throughout, and in part I want to tackle naturephilosophy in the context of contemporary ontology, particularly of the field ontology that Markus Gabriel has been doing such excellent work on, and the powers ontology that has become inescapable in contemporary metaphysics. If only they read Schelling. Naturephilosophy remains my concern not because I think nature is some vast thing that demands its ontological rights be recognized, but because it cannot be that what is is reducibly conceptual. Nature induces the descendental dimension into the powers of the concept, which is why thinking nature, or ontology, is always *kata dunamin*, as Plato constantly concludes, between the Idea and what is not it.

Credits

Cover image: Ring Nebula, otherwise known as Messier 57. 2500 light-years from earth, in the Lyra constellation. From the Hubble Telescope. Credit to NASA, ESA, and C. Robert O'Dell (Vanderbilt University). Original image in the public domain, edited by Kısmet Press, and republished under the same license. http://www.spacetelescope.org/images/heic1310a/.

Frontispiece: Created by Kısmet Press from: The Constellations (July, August, September), from Burritt's 1856 edition of the *Atlas to Illustrate the Geography of the Heavens*: https://commons.wikimedia.org/wiki/File:1856_Burritt_-_Huntington_Map_of_the_Constellations_or_Stars_in_July,_August_%5E_September_-_Geographicus_-_JulAugSep-burritt-1856.jpg; Thomas Curtis' 1829 *A London Encyclopaedia, or Universal Dictionary of Science, Art, Literature and Practical Mechanics*: https://commons.wikimedia.org/wiki/File:A_London_encyclopaedia,_or_universal_dictionary_of_science,_art,_literature_and_practical_mechanics_-_comprising_a_popular_view_of_the_present_state_of_knowledge_-_illustrated_by_numerous_engravings,_(14595451197).jpg; Albrecht Dürer (1471–1528), The Northern Celestial Hemisphere, woodcut, 1515, National Gallery of Art, 1515: https://commons.wikimedia.org/wiki/File:Albrecht_D%C3%BCrer_-_The_Northern_Celestial_Hemisphere_(NGA_1954.12.233).jpg

Albrecht_Dürer_-_The_Northern_Celestial_Hemisphere_ (NGA_1954.12.233). Original images all in the public domain, edited by Kısmet Press, and republished under the same license.

The interview with Iain Hamilton Grant was originally published in *Cosmos and History* Vol. 9, No. 2 (2013): 32–43, as "'Physics of the Idea': An Interview with Iain Hamilton Grant." It is republished here with kind permission of the editors, Paul Ashton and Arran Gare. The original version of the interview can be accessed at: http://cosmosandhistory.org/index.php/journal/article/view/377.

This book introduces the underlying ideas which have created the constellation of thought commonly referred to as Speculative Realism (SR). In a non-technical style *Speculative Realism: An Epitome* explores the thought of three contemporary philosophers: Quentin Meillassoux, Ray Brassier, and Iain Hamilton Grant. The book characterizes the milieu in which SR was born and charts how the tendencies of thought created from its birth have diverged into contemporary metaphysics. Readers will gain from the book an understanding how the evolving motion of concepts created by the brief life of SR continue to change speculative philosophy in the contemporary Continental philosophical landscape today.

Dr. Leon Niemoczynski is Visiting Assistant Professor of Philosophy at Moravian College in Bethlehem, Pennsylvania, United States. His research focuses mainly on the philosophy of nature, especially within the Continental philosophical tradition. He also maintains interests in a diverse range of topics including philosophical ecology, logic and metaphysics, German idealism, aesthetics, animal ethics, and the philosophy of religion. Philosophers most relevant to his current research include Plato, Hegel, Kant, Fichte, Schelling, Deleuze, and Merleau-Ponty. Niemoczynski is the author of *Speculative Naturalism* (forthcoming 2018); as co-editor, *Animal Experience: Consciousness and Emotions in the Natural World* (Open Humanities Press, 2014) and *A Philosophy of Sacred Nature: Prospects for Ecstatic Naturalism* (Lexington Books, 2014); and *Charles Sanders Peirce and a Religious Metaphysics of Nature* (Lexington Books, 2011). He currently resides in the Pocono Mountains of Northeastern, Pennsylvania with his wife, Nalina.

www.ingramcontent.com/pod-product-compliance
Lightning Source LLC
Chambersburg PA
CBHW050536300426
44113CB00012B/2134